Sinéad de Valera · Walter de la Mare
Ray Bradbury · Liam O'Flaherty
Shirley Jackson · James Thurber
Lord Dunsany · Robert Turner
Angelica Gibbs · Dal Stivens
William Saroyan · Katherine Mansfield

Twelve Short Masterpieces

Model Interpretations

By Klaus Burghardt and Douglas K. Stevenson

Ernst Klett Schulbuchverlag

Schülerbuch (weiße Seiten) herausgegeben von Klaus Burghardt und Rolf Eisenberg;
Lehrerbuch (blaue Seiten) von Klaus Burghardt und Dr. Douglas K. Stevenson.

The stories to which these interpretations refer are also available in a students' edition: *Twelve Short Masterpieces* (Klettbuch 5773).
The cassette accompanying this book contains the stories by Sinéad de Valera, Liam O'Flaherty, Shirley Jackson, James Thurber, Lord Dunsany and Dal Stivens (Klettnummer 57737).

1. Auflage 1 7 6 5 4 | 1995 94 93 92

Alle Drucke dieser Auflage können im Unterricht nebeneinander benutzt werden.
Die letzte Zahl bezeichnet das Jahr dieses Druckes.

Redaktion: Noreen O'Donovan und Dr. Hartmut K. Selke
Umschlaggestaltung: Hans Lämmle, Stuttgart.
Satz: Setzerei Lihs, Ludwigsburg.
Druck: Gutmann + Co., Heilbronn. Printed in Germany.

ISBN 3-12-577330-X

This book is dedicated to the memory of my friend and colleague Rolf Eisenberg, whose untimely death prevented him from witnessing the completion of the project he had initiated and contributed so much to. I would like to thank Dr. Stevenson for his willingness to finish the work in his place.

Klaus Burghardt

Contents

Introduction

This collection of stories and tales is intended mainly for young students who are just beginning to read English literature in the original version. For this reason, it has been restricted to really *short* stories, which can as a rule be read and understood at one sitting. This should ensure that little will get in the way of the reader's enjoyment of the stories.

Since the average length of the stories is so short, we have been able to include many different types of story – fairy tale, science fiction, crime, humour, etc. – told from a variety of angles and in widely differing styles. Thus this collection can function as an introductory course on *the art of storytelling*. For example, the reader will become aware of the various points of view from which a story can be told, can study how the various authors create atmosphere and suspense, and learn something about the relationship between fantasy and reality.

The majority of these stories centre around young people (children and young adults), either as main characters, or narrators, or both. For two reasons, it was relatively easy to find such stories for our collection. On the one hand, stories have always been told *to* children, to develop their imagination or to influence their behaviour (cf. our fairy tale). On the other hand, the problems associated with growing up and confronting the adult world have become favourite themes of modern short story writers.

In any case, the stories in our collection will provide plenty of opportunities for identification, whether with a legendary prince and princess, or with a young soldier in an imaginary future; with a teenage girl at her first dance, or even a seagull learning to fly. In addition, the messages hidden in these stories should provide plenty of material for discussion.

A Note to Teachers

Twelve Short Masterpieces contains enough material for a whole series of courses suitable for intermediate and advanced English classes. In the sequence presented here, the Teaching Units amount to an extensive treatment of the short story form in English and the art of storytelling in general. This full course assumes no previous experience in reading English literature in the original or expertise in interpreting stories, and gradually familiarizes the students with the most important concepts in literary criticism, enabling them at the same time to systematically analyse and compare stories representing a wide variety of genres and styles. But since most teachers will have less ambitious projects in mind, we have taken care to allow for a more flexible use of this Teacher's Book, and provide the information teachers need for constructing courses suited to the particular needs of their classes.

The table which follows (p. 11), for example, provides at a glance preliminary information on the content of each story, its genre, narrative technique, etc. This should suffice for the construction of thematic courses, such as:

Aggression and Violence 3, 5, 8, 9
Values 1, 3, 6, 8, 10
The Sexes 1, 6, 9, 11, 12
Generations 2, 4, 5, 10, 12

For courses based on particular aspects of literary technique teachers are advised to consult in addition the Index on page 182, since this specifies which aspects are actually dealt with, and in which of the Teaching Notes. Needless to say, any of the twelve stories can also be read on its own, for pure enjoyment, or to complement a course on a different topic.

For ease of orientation the Notes on each story begin with a summary of the contents and a brief evaluation of its most significant aspects. The Teaching Units themselves are, of course, in the nature of suggestions, which may need to be adapted to suit particular classes. Wherever possible we have taken care to point out alternative procedures, points which may be omitted or postponed, and even alternative interpretations of certain stories or parts of stories. Homework and group work assignments — set either as an integral part of the teaching strategy, or as optional extensions in the form of vocabulary work, creative writing, etc. — are intended to encourage independence and kindle the students' motivation.

In formulating answers to the comprehension, interpretation and discussion questions, we have not restricted vocabulary and syntax to what can be expected from classes at the intermediate level, but deliberately aimed at a judicious extension of the students' powers of expression, with regard to idiomatic phrasing and imagery, the use (where appropriate) of current literary terminology, and the forming of balanced sentences and paragraphs with the appropriate links and modifiers. It is up to each individual teacher to decide how much use can be made of the suggested wording without stifling spontaneity of expression.

A 'Listening Comprehension' phase based on the accompanying cassette has been incorporated into a number of the teaching sequences. This can of course be replaced by a different mode of presentation; suggestions are made in each case. But we do in any case strongly recommend the use of the cassette at some stage, e.g. at the end of the sequence, after any barriers to comprehension have been removed.

The circumstance that the short story form has flourished most strongly not in England itself, but on the Celtic 'fringe', in North America and in the Commonwealth countries, is reflected in this collection, and therefore in the accents of the speakers on the cassette. Their voices will help to establish some atmospheric contact with the linguistic and social background of each story, and develop the students' awareness of the variety of accents and standards of pronunciation which make up English as a world language. Advanced students may, in addition, attempt an analysis of the main differences, which are indicated in the table on page 181.

In spite of the variety of pronunciation to be heard on the cassette, the phonetic script used in the Annotations is that of the British standard most students are familiar with. For reasons of consistency and simplicity this principle has also been applied in the case of the stories by American authors, where the original American spelling has been retained. The following abbreviations are used in the Annotations:

Am.	American usage	*coll.*	colloquial
Austr.	Australian usage	*sl.*	slang
Gael.	Gaelic (Irish language)	*vulg.*	vulgar
Ger.	German language	*poet.*	poetic
usu.	usually	*arch.*	archaic

Numbers in bold-face type in the margin refer to the corresponding pages of the text, those in light-face type to the lines of the respective page. In the Teaching Notes, particular lines and passages in the stories are referred to by a similar system: e.g. **6** 7 = page 6 (of the students' book/white pages), line 7.

No.	Author/Title	Genre	Theme	Setting	Characters	Narrative Technique	Level of Difficulty
1	*Sinéad de Valera:* The Captive Princess	fairy tale	victory of good over evil	Ireland, legendary past	<u>young man,</u> wise woman, princess	3rd person narrative, 'omniscient' storyteller	easy
2	*Walter de la Mare:* The Riddle	ghost story/ cautionary tale	supernatural powers	old house in England, early 20th c.	<u>7 children,</u> grandmother	3rd person narrative, 'omniscient' author	medium
3	*Ray Bradbury:* A Piece of Wood	science fiction	war, technology, aggression	the future, a military post	<u>young soldier,</u> official	3rd person narrative, 'camera eye'	easy
4	*Liam O'Flaherty:* His First Flight	animal story	growing up, initiation	cliff, anywhere	<u>young seagull,</u> family	3rd person narrative, limited point of view	medium
5	*Shirley Jackson:* Charles	humour	the trials of parenthood	U.S., suburban home	mother, <u>son,</u> husband	1st person narrator (mother)	medium
6	*James Thurber:* The Princess and the Tin Box	parody (fairy tale)	real life vs. romantic notions	legendary past, some modern elements	<u>princess,</u> suitors	3rd person narrative, 'omniscient' storyteller	moderately difficult
7	*Lord Dunsany:* The Speech	mystery story	political intrigue and violence	London, pre-World War I	journalists, <u>politicians</u>	frame story: 3rd p. and 1st p. narrative	medium
8	*Robert Turner:* Christmas Gift	thriller	human feelings in a policeman's job	town in Florida	<u>policemen,</u> escaped convict	1st person narrator (older policeman)	medium
9	*Angelica Gibbs:* The Test	problem story	prejudice (racism, sexism)	town in U.S. (northern state)	<u>blackwoman,</u>employer, driving inspector	3rd person narrative, mainly 'camera eye'	medium
10	*Dal Stivens:* The Pepper-Tree	story of childhood	ambitions, dreams, resignation	Australia, suburban home	boy, <u>father,</u> mother	1st person narrator (boy as adult)	medium
11	*William Saroyan:* The Great Leapfrog Contest	story of childhood, humour	competitiveness among children	town in California	<u>boys,</u> a girl	1st person narrator (boy as adult)	medium
12	*Katherine Mansfield:* Her First Ball	story of initiation	transience of youth, initiation	New Zealand, turn of century	<u>girl,</u> friends, older man	3rd person narrator, limited point of view	moderately difficult

Sinéad de Valera

The Captive Princess

Years and years and years ago, when Fionn MacCool in Eirinn and Fionn Gall, a brother giant in Scotland, were building the Giant's Causeway, which was to run between the two countries, there lived in a glen in Antrim a young man named Hugh.

Everyone liked Hugh. He was very kind and neighbourly and it made him sad to see anyone in pain or trouble. He had also a great love for animals.

All the people in the place where Hugh lived had heard of an unhappy princess who had been carried off by a wicked giant and was kept a captive in his castle. This castle was a *crannog* or lake dwelling. It was built on stakes of wood driven down deep in the earth in the centre of the lake. The giant's wife was a witch and if anyone attempted to cross the lake, she set the water in motion and caused it to form whirlpools so that neither swimmer nor boat could reach the castle.

Hugh had a great desire to rescue the princess, whose name was Maca. One day he was sitting in his little house when he heard a wailing sound outside. He went to the door and saw a dog limping by, whining pitifully. He brought the dog into his house and saw that there was a large thorn in one of his front paws. He extracted the thorn and bathed the paw. The dog tried to thank him by licking his hand and then seemed to show that he wished Hugh to follow him. He led him some distance from his house and then turned down a narrow lane with high hedges on each side. At the end of the lane was a tiny little house. An old woman was sitting at the door. She looked very sad but when she saw the dog her face brightened. She thought he had been lost, he was so long away from her. The dog ran forward and put his head in her lap.

"I found this dog outside my house," said Hugh. "There was a thorn in his paw and when I took it out, he seemed to wish me to follow him."

"Good man," said the old woman, "and good dog. He wants me to befriend you as you have befriended him."

Now this old woman was a *bean feasa* (a woman of knowledge), that is, a woman with magic powers and with knowledge of things distant and hidden. She talked with Hugh for some time and he told her of his desire to rescue the princess.

"It is a hard task," said the old woman, "and there are many dangers in the way, but you are strong and brave and you will succeed if you follow my directions."

She went into the house and came out again with a large shell in her hand. Stretched across the shell were silver cords, something like the strings of a lute or violin. The old woman touched the strings and Hugh thought the music was the sweetest he had ever heard.

"Take this shell," said the old woman. "You will come to the Valley of Weasels. They will rush to swarm around you and attack you, but touch the strings lightly and they will become harmless. You will then come to a dark, dense wood through which it will be impossible to pass. Again, touch the strings and all will be well. Next, you must cross a deep, rugged quarry, but at the sound of the music your way will be clear. You have a long journey before you and you will need food."

Again she went into the house. She returned carrying a large oat cake.

"Take this," she said, "and my blessing with it."

"I shall never forget your kindness," said Hugh, as he set off with a stout heart.

It was not long before he reached the valley of weasels. They rushed towards him as if they would spring at this throat. Hugh drew his fingers across the strings of the shell. Immediately the weasels formed a line on each side of him and as he continued to play, they marched along with him till he passed out of the valley.

Next he came to the wood. The trees were so high and so close together that it was impossible for him to pass through. Hugh sounded the strings and all at once the branches parted and the trees themselves seemed to follow him till he came to the far end of the wood.

At last he reached the quarry. There were great jagged rocks on each side and a hollow in the middle. When he began to play, the stones from the bottom rose up and formed a smooth path for him and those at the sides moved gently with him till he reached the farther end.

He now sat down to rest near a clump of sloe bushes. As he was eating his oat cake, a tiny little bird fell from a robin's nest in the bush. He rose at once and gently placed the fledgling back in the nest.

Suddenly a little man stood before him. He had bright, twinkling eyes and a very friendly smile. He handed Hugh a feather, saying as he did so:

"For this your kindly deed
As on your way you speed,
Take this and in your need
'Twill serve you well.

By the side of the water which surrounds the giant's castle you will see a seagull. Strike the bird with this feather.

Now haste away,
Make no delay,
Ere close of day,
All will be well."

Having said this, the little man vanished.

Hugh continued his journey. After a time he again sat down to rest and eat some more of the cake. Just above him was an old oak tree with ivy climbing along the trunk. A bat had in some strange way got entangled in the ivy and could not move and there it remained, with the glaring sunshine hurting its poor eyes. Hugh climbed up the tree and placed the bat on the shady side, hidden by the ivy and protected by the branches of the oak.

Again he heard the words:

"For this your kindly deed,
As on your way you speed,
Take this and in your need,
'Twill serve you well."

There stood the little man, handing Hugh a bat's wing. "If you turn this around three times in your right hand, darkness thick as night will fall about you. This darkness will last for a short time only.

Now haste away,
Make no delay,
Ere close of day,
All will be well."

Like a flash the little man was gone.

When Hugh had travelled for some time, he sat down on a stone by the roadside. From the other side of the hedge came a sound as if some creature were in pain. He went through the hedge to the place from which the sound came. There he saw a cat down in a deep well and unable to climb out. Hugh took off his coat and, leaning over the edge of the well, lowered it towards the cat. Puss caught it with her forepaws and Hugh dragged her to safety.

"For this your kindly deed,
As on your way you speed,
Take this and in your need,
'Twill serve you well."

There stood the little man, handing Hugh a cat's eye. "Take this," he said, "and if you hold it in front of you, the darkest way will become bright and clear before you.

Now haste away,
Make no delay,
Ere close of day,
All will be well."

Again the little man disappeared.

Hugh journeyed on. After a time he came in sight of a huge stone castle built in the centre of a lake. This he knew to be the giant's home. At one of the top windows he caught sight of a beautiful, sad face and he knew that the Princess Maca was a captive there.

As Hugh came near the castle he saw the giant and his wife standing on the steps. When the pair saw Hugh, the giant waved his club round his head and the woman raised her wand over the water. Immediately it foamed and turned in all directions and formed whirlpools all round the castle.

Hugh felt it would be impossible to cross that dangerous lake but just then he saw perched on the bank beside him a beautiful seagull. Remembering the little man's advice, he struck the seagull with the feather. All at once the bird became so large and strong that Hugh mounted on its back and was carried across to the castle. When he descended from the back of the bird it flew up into the air.

The giant and his wife rushed down the steps but Hugh waved the bat's wing and in the darkness the pair lost their footing and fell headlong into the water. The whirlpools dragged them down, down and they were never heard of again.

By the light of the cat's eye, Hugh ascended the stairs to the room where the Princess Maca was. As he reached the door, the darkness disappeared and Hugh turned the key which was on the outside of the lock.

Maca told him she was the daughter of the King of Ulster.

"My father," said she, "banished from his kingdom a wicked giant. The giant's brother in revenge seized me and kept me imprisoned here."

"But," said Hugh, "how did the giant take you from your father's home? Are there not guards and attendants there?"

"Yes," said Maca, "but the giant found out that I liked to walk alone in a lovely wood which is near the palace. One spring day as I was gathering violets, he came and bore me away so quickly that I could not even call for help."

"Where is your father's castle?" Hugh asked.

"It is near the western coast and is so far away that I fear I shall never see my home again."

Hugh led the princess down to the water's edge. There stood the seagull. Hugh touched it with the feather. As he did it grew so large that he and

Maca were able to mount on its back. It flew westwards over lakes and plains, over hills and valleys, till it reached a beautiful glen in the midst of the blue hills of Donegal.

There stood the castle before them, its windows shining like gold in the rays of the setting sun.

They dismounted from the seagull and the bird flew swiftly away.

No words can describe the joy of the king and queen when they saw their daughter again. Maca told her parents all about her escape from the giant's castle and of Hugh's kindness and courage.

"You are a brave man," said the king, "and I should like to make you one of the chieftains of the kingdom."

"That would be a great honour," said Hugh, "and nothing would please me better except something which is almost too good to ask for."

"I know what that is," said the queen. "It is our daughter's hand in marriage."

Hugh looked at Maca.

She placed her hand in his, saying, "As I have already given you my heart, you may now take my hand."

The happy pair were married amid scenes of great rejoicing and lived happily ever after.

Biographical Notes

Sinéad Ó Flannagáin was born in a seaside town near Dublin in 1879. While studying to be a teacher, she met and married Eamon de Valera, who was a lecturer in mathematics at the time; he was one of the leaders of the fight for Irish independence, 1916–21, and later became President of the Republic.

Mrs de Valera showed a great patriotic interest in the survival of the Gaelic language. She was the author of several stories for children in Gaelic and also translated a number of children's books into this language.

In the fifties and sixties she published several collections of traditional stories in English: The Emerald Ring and Other Irish Fairy Tales, The Magic Girdle and Other Stories, *and* Fairy Tales of Ireland.

She died at the age of 96 in Dublin and is survived by five sons, two daughters, and numerous grandchildren.

Annotations

6 **Sinéad** [ʃɪ'ne:d] Gaelic form of 'Jane' or 'Janet' – **de Valera** [devə'leərə] – 1 **Fionn MacCool** ['fɪn mə'ku:l] – **Eirinn** ['e:rɪn] *Gael.* Ireland (dative case of 'Eire') – **Fionn Gall** ['fɪn'gɔ:l] *Gael.* (anglicized form: 'Fingal', as in 'Fingal's Cave') – 2 **giant** ['dʒaɪənt] (in fairy tales) person or creature of unusually great size – **causeway** ['kɔ:zweɪ] raised road across low ground or shallow water – **Giant's Causeway** a rock formation of crystallized lava on the north coast of Ireland (near Portrush) – 3 **glen** narrow valley (from *Gael.* 'gleann') – **Antrim** county in the North of Ireland – 4 **Hugh** [hju:] – 8 **wicked** ['wɪkɪd] morally bad – **captive** ['kæptɪv] prisoner – 9 **crannog** [krɑ'no:g/'krænəg] *Gael.* – **dwelling** house, residence – 10 **stake** pole – 11 **witch** Hexe – **to set in motion** to start moving – 12 **whirlpool** ['wɜ:lpu:l] water moving rapidly in a circle – 14 **Maca** ['mɔkə] – 15 **to wail** to utter a long cry of pain or suffering – 16 **to limp** to walk unevenly because of a hurt or stiff leg – **to whine** to make a high, sad sound – 18 **paw** foot of an animal (with claws) – **to extract** to pull out – 21 **lane** narrow road, path – 25 **lap** Schoß – 30 **bean feasa** ['ban'fasə] *Gael.*

7 4 **shell** hard covering of a small sea animal – 6 **lute** [lu:t] stringed musical instrument (Laute) – 9 **weasel** small thin animal with a thick fur – 11 **dense** [dens] thick – 12 **rugged** ['rʌgɪd] *here:* wild and rocky – **quarry** [ɒ] large man-made hole from which stone is obtained (Steinbruch) – 15 **oat cake** cake or bread made of oats (Hafer) – 17 **stout** *here:* brave – 26 **to part** to spread apart, leaving a space in the middle – 28 **jagged** ['dʒægɪd] rough and with sharp edges – 29 **hollow** ['hɒləʊ] *(n.)* hole, piece of lower ground – 30 **smooth** [ð] flat, not rough – 32 **sloe** [sləʊ] Schlehe – 33 **robin** songbird with a red breast – 34 **fledgling** young bird – 37 **deed** a thing done – 40 **'twill** = it will

8 2 **seagull** common white seabird – 3 **to haste** [heɪst] to hurry – 5 **ere** *poet.* before – 7 **to vanish** to disappear – 9 **oak** Eiche – **ivy** ['aɪvɪ] evergreen climbing plant (Efeu) – 10 **trunk** the main stem of a tree – **bat** small, mouselike flying animal (Fledermaus) – **to get entangled** to get caught (in) – 11 **to glare** to shine unpleasantly bright – 28 **creature** ['kri:tʃə] – 30 **well** hole drilled into the earth for obtaining water – 32 **Puss** child's name for a cat

9 11 **club** heavy stick with one thick end – 12 **wand** [ɒ] stick with magic powers (Zauberstab) – **to foam** to form bubbles – 15 **to perch** (of a bird) to sit or rest on s.th. – **bank** land beside a lake or river – 17 **to mount** to get up on – 18 **to descend** [dɪ'send] to come down – 21 **to lose one's footing** to stumble, to lose one's balance – **headlong** head first, falling without control – 24 **to ascend** [ə'send] to climb, to go up – 27 **Ulster** northern province of Ireland – 28 **to banish** to send out of the country as a punishment – 29 **to seize** [si:z] to catch, to carry away by force – 31 **attendant** servant – 34 **to bear (bore, borne)** to carry – **violet** ['vaɪələt] small dark-blue flower (Veilchen)

10 3 **Donegal** ['dʌnɪgɔ:l] county in the north-west of Ireland – 5 **ray** narrow beam of light – **to set** (of the sun) to sink below the horizon – 6 **swift** quick – 11 **chieftain** ['tʃi:ftən] leader of a tribe or clan – 19 **amid** among, surrounded by – **rejoicing** activities expressing happiness and joy

Interpretation and Teaching Notes

Summary and Analysis

This story is set in prehistoric Ireland, which has provided Celtic storytellers through the ages with a rich supply of legends and lore. The introductory passage makes an explicit link with other such tales, thus stressing the storyteller's credentials and giving this story an air of plausibility. The story tells of a kind, neighbourly young man named Hugh, who is filled with the desire to rescue Maca, a princess kept prisoner by a giant in a huge stone castle in the middle of a lake whose waters are turned into whirlpools by the magic of the giant's wife.

One day after Hugh has pulled out a thorn from a dog's paw he is led by the animal to an old woman's house. She turns out to be a kind of 'good fairy' and presents Hugh with a shell with silver strings to help him to free the princess. The music of the instrument is meant to lead him safely through the dangerous Valley of the Weasels, an impassable dense wood, and a deep rugged quarry. Also supplied with a large oat cake and the woman's blessings, Hugh sets off and overcomes the first three obstacles.

Continuing his journey, Hugh rescues the lives of a robin, a bat, and a cat. Each time a little man appears and rewards him for his kindness: Hugh is handed a bird's feather, a bat's wing, and a cat's eye, all of which will help to break the power of the giant and his wife.

When Hugh approaches the whirling water of the lake, he remembers the little man's advice. He touches a seagull with the feather. Immediately the bird becomes large and strong and carries him across to the castle. Next the magic of the bat's wing wraps the two giants in darkness and makes them fall into the water. By the light of the cat's eye Hugh reaches the princess's room and frees her.

On the seagull's back Hugh and Maca return to the king's castle. For his kindness and courage, Maca's father offers to make Hugh one of his chieftains, but Hugh prefers to ask for his daughter's hand. Maca and her parents consent and the happy pair are married.

As this summary shows, the plot can be said to concentrate on an illustration of Hugh's remarkable kindness, his love for animals, and his courage. A clear division is made between good and evil, with the former drawing much of its strength from a sympathetic alliance between young and old, man and animal. It is this alliance which in the end carries the victory over the 'black magic' of the giant's wife. (**6** 11–13; **9** 11–12) In this fight, the good side commands supernatural powers as well. Its magic power, however, is used in a just cause and acquired only after a series of successful trials, as it were, and so is clearly marked off from the destructive witchcraft of the giant's wife.

As in most such fairy tales, the hero's character is presented in outline only. It does not change during the progress of the narration. In fact, our steadfast hero is as much a stereotype as the 'unhappy princess' or the 'wicked giant' (**6** 7, 8), but one the listeners are expected to identify with, and model themselves on.

To heighten the listener's suspense and to accentuate the moral lesson, the narrator has worked in a number of delaying episodes, each a variation on the same theme. The two sets of three almost identical episodes (Hugh's brave march through valley, wood and quarry, and the three appearances of the little man) also serve to give the story a shape which can be immediately appreciated.

Maca's deliverance, the climax of an uncomplicated and straightforward narrative, is dealt with in a few dramatic lines (**9** 10–26). The briefness of the actual fight once more underlines the moral of the tale, i.e. that evil cannot survive a challenge from those strengthened by the moral principles of pity and love. Accordingly, the closing section of the tale reconfirms Hugh's morality. Maca's love matters more to Hugh that the prospect of a chieftancy in her father's kingdom. So, as in all good fairy tales, they live "happily ever after".

Unit I
Listening Comprehension

Introductory Remarks:

— For an oral presentation most appropriate to the 'fairy tale' genre, we recommend the use of the recording (Klettnummer 57737). Alternatively, the teacher could read the story to the class.
— If the recording is not available, and the teacher does not wish to take on the role of 'storyteller', the following procedure can also apply to a first reading of the story by the students in class.

1. First paragraph (**13** 1–4): Establishment of setting and atmosphere, 'suspension of disbelief'

What did you not understand?
[Clarify difficulties with the help of the annotations. If necessary, play this section of the recording again.]
What is the opening phrase, and what does it tell you?
With the phrase "years and years ago..." the storyteller leads us from the present to a distant past. The reference is very vague, however, just like the even more common fairy-tale formula "once upon a time...". Such a formula sets the mood for the wildest fantasy, in other words, it causes the reader to 'suspend disbelief'.
What about the reference to the two giants?
A number of points are relevant:
— This reference makes it clear that the story is set in the world of myth and legend, and not necessarily in a historical past.
— The two giants are popular characters in Gaelic folklore. This establishes a connection with other Gaelic tales (e.g. the building of the Giant's Causeway) and thus gives the impression that the storyteller/narrator knows what she is talking about.
What about the reference to real places?
[A map showing the north of Ireland and Scotland might prove useful here. If the slide series *Dias zur Landeskunde, Reihe 5: Ireland,* (Klettnummer 56815) is available, slide 30 could be shown.]
The reference to real places — Scotland, Ireland, Antrim — is probably unnecessary in a fairy tale, but it adds a certain illusion of reality. The "Giant's Causeway" is also a real place, whether you accept the legend about its origin or not.

2. Second and third paragraphs (**6** 5–13): Main characters, basic situation.
What people are mentioned, and what are you told about them?
Hugh — likeable, kind, neighbourly, loves animals; obviously the hero of the story;
Princess — unhappy, captive in giant's castle;
Giant – wicked;
Witch (giant's wife) — magic powers used to keep princess captive.
What impression are you given of the castle?
There is no real description of the castle — the storyteller's 'picture' consists of a few bold strokes, presenting only those elements which make it clear just how difficult it would be to free the princess.
For those who know that there is archeological evidence for the existence of such lake dwellings, this also adds to the illusion of reality (see point 1).

3. Expectations aroused by this 'exposition'
What do you think will happen in the story?
[Free discussion. The students' answers will be based on their own experience of fairy tales. The outcome is easy to guess, less so the means by which the freeing of the princess will be achieved.]

4. Oral presentation of whole story.
[It should be made clear that the students are not expected to understand every detail, but just to get the gist of the story.]

5. Discussion of initial reactions
How much did you understand of the story?
What made it easy/difficult to understand?
Say whether you liked the story, and why.

Homework: Read the story at home, in order to be able to discuss the details.

Unit II
The Structure of the Plot

1. Comprehension Questions
What does Hugh want to do? (**6** 14)
What kind of person is the old woman? (**6** 30–31)
Why does she help Hugh? (**6** 15–29)
How does Hugh overcome the first three dangerous obstacles? (**7** 19–31)
What else happens on Hugh's journey?
[This question requires a summing up of three separate episodes of similar structure, so a full answer is given.]
After having sat down to rest at various places and to eat from the *bean feasa*'s cake, Hugh rescues the lives of a helpless tiny bird, a blinded bat, and a drowning cat. Each time a little man appears to reward Hugh for his kindness. Wishing him well, the little man hands him a bird's feather, a bat's wing, and a cat's eye together with some advice on how to rescue the princess by means of the magic that is connected with these things.
How does Hugh make use of the little man's gifts? (**9** 6–26)
What does he find out about the princess? (**9** 27–38)
How is Hugh rewarded for rescuing the princess? (**10** 10–20)

2. Divisions in the narrative

Examine the way the events that make up the story are presented. Mark the main sections of the story, and think up a heading for each.

[Allow 5—10 minutes for this exercise — group work possible.]

6 1–14:	Introduction/Exposition.
6 15–25:	Hugh's good deed.
6 26–**7** 18:	The *bean feasa's* gratitude/The *bean feasa* helps him on his way.
7 19–31:	The three obstacles at the beginning of Hugh's journey.
7 32–**9** 5:	Hugh continues his journey: three more good deeds are rewarded. *or* The little man's three appearances: Hugh is rewarded for his good deeds.
9 6–26:	Hugh defeats the giant and witch, and enters the castle.
9 27–38:	The princess's story.
9 39–**10** 6:	Hugh takes the princess home.
10 7–20:	Hugh's reward/The gratitude of Maca and her parents.

The above suggestion presents a maximum number of subdivisions, which can be reduced. The minimum would be three main sections: Preparation for the journey — Hugh overcomes all difficulties and succeeds in his quest — The happy ending.

3. The journey as unifying factor

Lots of different things happen in the story. What holds it all together?

Unlike many modern short stories, this tale does not offer 'unity of place'. Though all of the events take place somewhere in the north of Ireland (and most of them in one day), the storyteller stresses the idea of movement. Starting from the "glen in Antrim" (**6** 3), it is a "long journey" (**7** 13) through the "Valley of Weasels" (**7** 19), the dense wood (**7** 24), the rugged quarry (**7** 28) and on towards the giant's castle. The passage of time is mentioned again and again (**8** 8, 27; **9** 6). But all of this movement is held together by the idea of Hugh's quest, i.e. his journey in pursuit of an important aim. Everything that happens is in some way a test of his goodness or courage.

4. Suspense

Most listeners will realize at an early stage that the story will have a happy ending. How does the storyteller manage to keep your attention in spite of this?

It may be obvious that Hugh will succeed in his quest, but one is not sure how. At each turn in the plot, i.e. at each stage of his journey, the listener/reader is confronted with a new uncertainty:

— Will the *bean feasa's* magic lute really work?
— Will Hugh be brave enough to face the dangers?
— How will the little man's gifts help Hugh?
— How will Hugh get across the foaming lake? — etc.

At what point in the story does the suspense build up to a climax?
The climax of the story is the confrontation between Hugh and the evil characters, the giant and his wife (**9** 14–23). After this the listener can relax — the forces of evil have been defeated.
The second time you heard/read the story, you knew what would happen. Did this spoil it for you?
Individual answers will vary. Some will share the enjoyment children feel on hearing a familiar story repeated. Much of this satisfaction comes from being reassured that good will triumph over evil.

Homework: Pick out those passages where Hugh's character is tested.

Unit III
A Typical Fairy Tale?

1. The moral: triumph of good over evil
What would you say is the moral of the story?
Evidently, the story's message is an affirmation of a clearcut moral concept: the forces of evil, powerful and menacing as they may appear, cannot survive a serious challenge by the forces of good. Hugh's kindness is rewarded with everlasting happiness (**10** 19–20) and the evil giant and witch suffer ignominious defeat (**9** 20–23) and are condemned to fall into oblivion.
How does Hugh prove that he deserves to succeed? [Discussion of Homework]
Before he is able to fulfil his desire, Hugh is put to a number of trials, all testing the quality of his character. Several times Hugh has to prove his kindness and love of animals (**6** 15–25; **7** 32–34; **8** 10–13, 28–33) and with it his resoluteness and courage (**7** 1–3, 19–31; **9** 14–23). Finally, Hugh has to choose between the sure reward of worldy power (**10** 10–13) and the risk of falling into the king's disgrace by daring, as a common villager, to ask for Maca's hand in marriage (**10** 12–13).
What other fairy tales do you know? Is the moral similar?

[Though it will suffice to compare this story with some well-known German *Märchen*, those who wish to consider other fairy tales in English will find three interesting examples under the heading "Folk Tales" in *Great Fantasy Stories* (Klettnummer 5772).]

Apart from the moral, what else has this story got in common with the other fairy tales you know?

[Free discussion; the similarities found will, of course, depend on the stories which are compared, but the following points should be touched on.]

2. Elements of magic and the supernatural:

— Mythical creatures (giants, 'little people' etc.) exist side by side with ordinary mortals like Hugh.

— The forces of good and evil possess an impressive arsenal of supernatural 'weapons' (**6** 10; **7** 4–14; **8** 1–2, 19–21, 38–40; **9** 10–**10** 3).

3. Stylistic features typical of the fairy tale:

— The use of stereotyped opening and closing formulae. "Years and years ago" (**6** 1) is a variant of the even more familiar "Once upon a time". The story ends with the classic phrase "(they) lived happily ever after".

— The repetition of important phrases (here, verses: **7–9**) in a series of similar situations is typical of fairy tales. This intensifies the impression of structural compactness and underlines the dramatic significance of each episode. The verses can also be remembered as a sort of moral guideline after the tale has been told.

— The frequent embellishment of nouns with adjectives which either add to the atmosphere (e.g. **6** 21–22, **7** 10–13) or stress the moral absolutes of the story (e.g. **6** 8).

4. The intended audience

Who do you think the tale is told to?

The innocent view of life which is expressed in the story suggests that it is aimed at a rather young audience, maybe children below the age of seven. But they are certainly not the only people who may find a clearcut moral attractive or consoling. The mythical setting at the beginning of the tale as well as the romantic light into which the geography of the north of Ireland is dipped may also meet the taste of older children and even adults.

Additional Homework [Optional; can be expanded to a full unit if desired]:
Note down all words and phrases referring to

a) nature (animals, plants, etc.);

b) feelings and character.

Walter de la Mare

The Riddle

So these seven children, Ann, and Matilda, James, William and Henry, Harriet and Dorothea, came to live with their grandmother. The house in which their grandmother had lived since her childhood was built in the time of the Georges. It was not a pretty house, but roomy, substantial, and square; and an elm tree outstretched its branches almost to the windows.

When the children were come out of the cab (five sitting inside and two beside the driver), they were shown into their grandmother's presence. They stood in a little black group before the old lady, seated in her bow window. And she asked them each their names, and repeated each name in her kind, quavering voice. Then to one she gave a work-box, to William a jack-knife, to Dorothea a painted ball; to each a present according to age. And she kissed all her grandchildren to the youngest.

"My dears," she said, "I wish to see all of you bright and gay in my house. I am an old woman, so that I cannot romp with you; but Ann must look to you, and Mrs Fenn too. And every morning and every evening you must all come in to see your granny; and bring me smiling faces, that call back to my mind my own son Harry. But all the rest of the day, when school is done, you shall do just as you please, my dears. And there is only one thing, just one, I would have you remember. In the large spare bedroom that looks out on the slate roof there stands in the corner an old oak chest; ay, children, older than I, my dears, a great deal older; older than my grandmother. Play anywhere else in the house, but not there." She spoke kindly to them all, smiling at them; but she was very aged, and her eyes seemed to see nothing of this world.

And the seven children, though at first they were gloomy and strange, soon began to be happy and at home in the great house. There was much to interest and to amuse them there; all was new to them. Twice every day, morning and evening, they came in to see their grandmother, who every day seemed more feeble; and she spoke pleasantly to them of her mother, and her childhood, but never forgetting to visit her store of sugar-plums. And so the weeks passed by.

It was evening twilight when Henry went upstairs from the nursery by himself to look at the oak chest. He pressed his fingers into the carved fruit and flowers, and spoke to the dark smiling heads at the corners; and then, with a glance over his shoulder, he opened the lid and looked in. But the chest concealed no treasure, neither gold nor baubles, nor was there anything to alarm the eye. The chest was empty, except that it was lined with silk of old rose, seeming darker in the dusk, and smelling sweet of potpourri. And while Henry was looking in, he heard the softened laughter and the clinking of the cups downstairs in the nursery; and out at the window he saw the day darkening. These things brought strangely to his memory his mother, who in her glimmering white dress used to read to him in the dusk; and he climbed into the chest; and the lid closed gently down over him.

When the other six children were tired with their playing, they filed into their grandmother's room as usual for her goodnight and her sugar-plums. She looked out between the candles at them as if she were unsure of something in her thoughts. The next day Ann told her grandmother that Henry was not anywhere to be found.

"Dearie me, child. Then he must be gone away for a time," said the old lady. She paused. "But remember all of you, do not meddle with the oak chest."

But Matilda could not forget her brother Henry, finding no pleasure in playing without him. So she would loiter in the house thinking where he might be. And she carried her wood doll in her bare arms, singing under her breath all she could make up about him. And when in a bright morning she peeped in on the chest, so sweet-scented and secret it seemed that she took her doll with her into it – just as Henry himself had done.

So Ann, and James, and William, Harriet and Dorothea were left at home to play together. "Some day maybe they will come back to you, my dears," said their grandmother, "or maybe you will go to them. Heed my warning as best you may."

Now Harriet and William were friends together, pretending to be sweethearts; while James and Dorothea liked wild games of hunting, and fishing, and battles.

On a silent afternoon in October Harriet and William were talking softly together, looking out over the slate roof at the green fields, and they heard the squeak and frisking of a mouse behind them in the room. They went together and searched for the small, dark hole from whence it had come out. But finding no hole, they began to finger the carving of the chest, and to give names to the dark-smiling heads, just as Henry had done. "I know! Let's pretend you are Sleeping Beauty, Harriet," said William, "and I'll be the Prince that squeezes through the thorns and comes in." Harriet looked gently and strangely at her brother; but she got into the box and lay down, pretending to be fast asleep; and on tiptoe William leaned over, and seeing how big was the chest he stepped in to kiss the Sleeping Beauty and to wake her from her quiet sleep. Slowly the carved lid turned on its noiseless hinges. And only the clatter of James and Dorothea came in sometimes to recall Ann from her book.

But their old grandmother was very feeble, and her sight dim, and her hearing extremely difficult.

Snow was falling through the still air upon the roof; and Dorothea was a fish in the oak chest, and James stood over the hole in the ice, brandishing a walking-stick for a harpoon, pretending to be an Esquimau. Dorothea's face was red, and her wild eyes sparkled through her tousled hair. And James had a crooked scratch upon his cheek. "You must struggle, Dorothea, and then I shall swim back and drag you out. Be quick now!" He shouted with laughter as he was drawn into the open chest. And the lid closed softly and gently down as before.

Ann, left to her self, was too old to care overmuch for sugar-plums, but she would go solitary to bid her grandmother goodnight; and the old lady looked wistfully at her over her spectacles. "Well, my dear," she said with trembling head; and she squeezed Ann's fingers between her own knuckled finger and thumb. "What lonely old people we are, to be sure!" Ann kissed her grandmother's soft, loose cheek. She left the old lady sitting in her easy chair, her hands upon her knees, and her head turned sidelong towards her.

When Ann was gone to bed she used to sit reading her book by candle-light. She drew up her knees under the sheets, resting her book upon them. Her story was about fairies and gnomes; and the gently-flowing moonlight of the narrative seemed to illumine the white pages, and she could hear in fancy fairy voices, so silent was the great many-roomed house, and so mellifluent were the words of the story. Presently she put out her candle, and, with a confused babel of voices close to her ears, and faint swift pictures before her eyes, she fell asleep.

And in the dead of night she arose out of bed in dream, and with eyes wide open yet seeing nothing of reality, moved silently through the vacant house. Past the room where her grandmother was snoring in brief, heavy slumber, she stepped light and surely, and down the wide staircase. And Vega the far-shining stood over against the window above the slate roof. Ann walked in the strange room as if she were being guided by the hand toward the oak chest. There, just as if she was dreaming it was her bed, she laid herself down in the old rose silk, in the fragrant place. But it was so dark in the room that the movement of the lid was indistinguishable.

Through the long day, the grandmother sat in her bow window. Her lips were pursed, and she looked with dim, inquisitive scrutiny upon the street where people passed to and fro, and vehicles rolled by. At evening she climbed the stair and stood in the doorway of the large spare bedroom. The ascent had shortened her breath. Her magnifying spectacles rested upon her nose. Leaning her hand on the doorpost she peered in towards the glimmering square of window in the quiet gloom. But she could not see far, because her sight was dim and the light of day feeble. Nor could she detect the faint fragrance, as of autumnal leaves. But in her mind was a tangled skein of memories – laughter and tears, and little children now old-fashioned, and the advent of friends, and long farewells. And gossiping fitfully, inarticulately, with herself, the old lady went down again to her window-seat.

Biographical Notes

Walter de la Mare, English poet, novelist, essayist and critic, was born in Kent in 1873 of a Scottish Huguenot family. He attended St. Paul's Cathedral Choir School, London, where he founded and edited a school-magazine.

After leaving school he worked for eighteen years as a clerk in the London offices of the Anglo-American Standard Oil Company. During these years he published some short stories, a volume of verse and a novel. When he was granted a small pension from the British Government in 1908, he was able to direct all his attention to writing.

His talent as a poet was widely recognized after the publication of The Listeners and Other Poems *in 1912. He became really well known when his novel* Memoirs of a Midget *(1921) won the Tait Black Memorial Prize for 1922. Besides that he was awarded a number of other literary prizes for his novels and poems.*

In his later life he received several honorary university degrees and public honours. He died in 1956.

Walter de la Mare is widely known as a poet of gentle fantasy and is regarded by many as the supreme poet of childhood. There is no doubt about his great skill in creating atmosphere. His poems are full of half-heard whispers, moonlight, and mystery. His novels and short stories again and again deal with the supernatural and the macabre.

Annotations

13 4 **the Georges** the Kings from George I to George IV (1714–1830) – 5 **elm tree** large, tall tree with broad leaves (Ulme) – 6 **cab** *here:* horse-drawn carriage (modern meaning: taxi) – 8 **bow window** curved window forming an alcove – 10 **to quaver** to tremble from weakness – **work-box** container for small things needed for sewing, such as needles and thread – 11 **jack-knife** small folding knife – 14 **to romp** to play noisily with a lot of running and jumping – 20 **slate** flat, thin grey stone (Schiefer) – **oak** large tree with hard wood (Eiche) – **chest** large wooden box – 25 **gloomy** sad, depressed – 29 **feeble** weak, as from old age – 30 **store** collection of things put aside for later use – 32 **nursery** room in which children can play – 33 **to carve** to form by cutting away the surrounding wood or stone

14 3 **to conceal** [–'–] to hide – **bauble** cheap jewel – 4 **to line s.th.** to cover the inside of s.th. (with cloth) – 5 **dusk** time just before it gets quite dark – **pot-pourri** [ˌpəʊ'pʊəri] mixture of dried pieces of sweet-smelling flowers and leaves kept in a jar – 9 **glimmering** shining – 11 **to file** to walk one after the other – 17 **do not meddle with** stay away from – 20 **to loiter** to stand or move about aimlessly – 23 **to peep** to look at s.th. quickly and secretly – **sweet-scented** smelling sweet – 27 **to heed** to pay attention to – 34 **to frisk** to run and jump about playfully – 38 **Sleeping Beauty** Dornröschen – 39 **to squeeze** (through) to force oneself through

15 4 **hinge** [hɪndʒ] metal part on which a lid or door turns or swings – 6 **dim (sight)** bad eyesight – 9 **to brandish** to wave around in the air; to swing – 10 **Esquimau** ['eskɪməʊ] also spelt 'Eskimo' – 11 **to sparkle** to send out little flashes of light – **tousled** [aʊ] untidy; in disorder – 12 **crooked** ['krʊkɪd] not straight – 17 **solitary** quite alone; without friends – 18 **wistful** melancholy – 19 **knuckled** *here:* bent at the knuckles (Knöchel) – 21 **easy chair** armchair – 25 **fairy, gnome** [nəʊm] small, imaginary beings – 28 **mellifluent** [me'lɪflʊənt] *usu.* **mellifluous** sweet-sounding – 29 **babel** ['beɪbəl] mixture of voices which are impossible to understand – 32 **vacant** ['veɪkənt] empty – 35 **Vega** name of a star – 38 **fragrant** ['freɪgrənt] sweet-smelling; *noun:* **fragrance** – 39 **indistinguishable** impossible to see (a difference, a movement etc.)

16 2 **to purse (lips)** to press one's lips together – **inquisitive** [ɪŋ'kwɪzɪtɪv] curious, wanting to know s.th. – **scrutiny** ['skru:tɪnɪ] close and very careful look – 5 **ascent** climb, upward movement – **(magnifying) spectacles** glasses – 6 **to peer** to look closely at s.th. that is difficult to see – 7 **gloom** darkness – 9 **tangled skein** [skeɪn] confused mass (of threads) – 11 **advent** ['– –] arrival – **to gossip** *here:* to talk a lot about unimportant things (usually about other people) – **fitfully** restlessly – **inarticulately** [ˌɪnɑ:'tɪkjʊlətlɪ] not speaking clearly

Interpretation and Teaching Notes

Summary and Analysis

Significantly, this story begins with a suggestion of things left unsaid. For some unexplained reason, seven children come to live with their aged grandmother in her roomy Georgian house. After she has kissed them welcome, she lays down some rules of conduct: Every morning and evening, the children are expected to come into their grandmother's room with smiling faces to call back to her mind her own (presumably dead) son Harry. After school they are free to play anywhere in the house except in the large spare bedroom where there is an old oak chest.

Henry is the first to break this rule. One morning he takes a furtive glance at the beautifully carved and sweet-smelling chest. When he climbs into the empty box, the lid closes over him. The next day, when the old lady is informed about Henry's disappearance, she merely states that he must be gone for a time and repeats her order not to meddle with the chest.

But one morning Matilda, in search of her brother, climbs into the chest with her doll and disappears like Henry before her. Once again, the old lady repeats her half-hearted warning. Harriet and William are the next to be trapped by the noiseless lid of the chest while using it to play 'Sleeping Beauty'. Then, James and Dorothea fall victim to the strange chest while they are using it for a wild Eskimo game.

Finally, one night, after reading a fairy tale, Ann sleepwalks through the vacant house to the oak chest in the bedroom. Dreaming it is her bed, she lies down in it and shares the fate of the other six children.

The story ends with the old lady left alone with her memories. She too, looks into the room with the mysterious chest in it, but her bad eyesight prevents her from seeing much. Talking restlessly to herself, the old lady returns to her window-seat.

After a first cursory reading of de la Mare's story, it might seem to be one of the numerous 'cautionary tales' for little children which enjoyed great popularity in Victorian England and in the first decades of the 20th century. In the present story, the children repeatedly neglect the orders of their grandmother (**13** 18–22; **14**, 16–18, 27–28). Punishment follows in the wake, but the mysterious disappearance of their playmates does not make them wiser. Still, it would be a mistake to regard de la Mare as an advocate of harsh Victorian or Edwardian educational principles.

On closer scrutiny, it becomes evident in how subtle a way de la Mare has transformed the moral of those 'cautionary tales'. Instead of a clear-cut definition of good and bad, right and wrong, we have ambivalence and mystery. As regards the old lady, the combination of overt kindness with indifference borders on the sinister. As regards the children, their disobedience is a product of powerful impulses over which they have no control – whether these impulses are of natural or supernatural origin, or (as is strongly suggested) a combination of both. One sympathizes strongly with these seven orphans, imprisoned, as it were, in this strange old house and thrown back upon the reservoir of their memories or upon the power of their imagination. It is probably no coincidence that their games with the oak chest are mentioned in connection with the window of this very bedroom which gives on to the world outside (**14** 7–8, 32–34, etc.), as if their memories, fantasies and make-believe were the key to their freedom. But instead they are led to the oak chest, which turns out to be a fatal trap. Or is it? This depends on where they have gone, a question the story does not answer.

It is worth noting that the situation of the children bears a strong resemblance to that of their aging grandmother. The bow window likewise separates the old lady from the pulse of time (**16** 1–3) and her memories gradually take over her whole consciousness; she seems to "see nothing of this world" (**13** 23–24). Unlike the children, however, she will not need a mysterious oak chest to spirit her out of this world. Significantly, the physical decay of the old woman is running parallel to the mysterious disappearance of her grandchildren (**14** 13–14; **15** 6–7, 18–20; **16** 4–9).

The supernatural requisite of the narrative, the oak chest, brings the tale closer to the traditional 'ghost story' than to the 'cautionary tale'. Though no ghosts are seen, the atmosphere conjured up by the narrative — twilight, gloom, candles, faint moonlight and a mysterious fragrance — strongly suggests their presence. The oak chest seems to be the point where a strange, sunken world of spirits impinges on 'reality'.

Whether the children are being drawn by the mysterious power of the chest to join their dead parents in this other world (as strongly suggested in the lines **14** 8–10) or whether there is some even more sinister explanation, is a matter for speculation. The story remains what the author says it is, a "riddle".

Preparatory Steps

Since the reader of this mysterious story is meant to be puzzled, a general introduction in class is advisable, to avoid the students attributing any puzzlement to their own inadequacies. This could be done in 10–20 minutes, as follows:

1. Read the first sentence.
What does it tell you?
What does it not *tell you?*
What does the first word indicate?
The main point is that you are not told *why* the children came to live with their grandmother. The word 'so' at the beginning gives the impression that this is only the continuation of a much longer story – we are left guessing what went before. This will be true of other things in the story as well.

2. Read the rest of the first paragraph.
What is the setting of the story?/In what way does the setting of this story differ from the fairy tale you have just read?
Unlike the fairy tale, this story seems to have a very realistic setting: England in the early 20th century, 'the present' for the author. The details given about the house make it seem very solid and real.

To sum up: The setting is realistic, so you do not expect fairies and witches, but real people and real events. But some things are not told, so be prepared for surprises!

Homework: Read the whole story.

Unit I
Strange Happenings in an Old House

1. Comprehension (plot)
Where does the story take place?
(**13** 2–5, 19–20; **14** 32–33; **16** 1–3)
What kind of welcome are the children given by their grandmother?
(**13** 6–12)
How does she want them to behave towards her?
(**13** 13–18)

What does the old lady tell them about the oak chest?
(**13** 18–22)
What does Henry find out about the chest?
(**13** 33–**14** 6)
What happens to the children one by one?
(**14** 6–10, 19–24; **14** 32; **15** 4; **15** 8–15, 31–39)
How does the old lady respond to her grandchildren's successive disappearance?
(**14** 11–18, 26–28; **15** 17–20)
What happens after all seven children have disappeared from their grandmother's home?
(**16** 1–12)

2. The description of the old house
What are you told about the old house? What details are stressed?
For some reason, the writer must not have been interested in giving a detailed description of the place. The opening paragraph offers only some general information concerning the age, structure and size of the house. Interestingly, the position of the elm tree is almost given the same attention as the building itself (**13** 5), though it will not be mentioned again in the story.
As far as the interior of this "great many-roomed house" is concerned (**15** 27), two details come into prominence: the bow window (**13** 8–9; **16** 1–3) which overlooks the street and the "large spare bedroom" (upstairs) with the oak chest in one of its corners (**13** 19–20, 23, etc.). The room has got a square window (**16** 7) which gives on to a "slate roof" (**13** 20) behind which there is a stretch of "green fields" (**14** 33). Greater efforts have been made to describe the mysterious oak chest (**13** 33–**14** 10). It is decorated with "carved fruit and flowers", and there are "dark smiling heads at the corner". Inside it is lined with silk of sweet-smelling old rose (**14** 4–6). According to the old lady, the chest is "older than [her] grandmother" (**13** 2).
What impression do you get from the descriptions of the house and the chest?
The vague description of the house is clearly at odds with the amount of information about the chest in the bedroom. Though this Georgian house is square and solid, its indistinct geography will probably prevent a sensitive reader from feeling at home in it. One gets the feeling that it is a rather sinister place. What is more, one's uneasiness is likely to grow, with the very detailed description of the chest; none of the details seem to offer the slightest clue to its secret.

3. Unanswered questions
A lot of things are left untold in this story. Make a list of them in the form of questions.
[This can be either a written exercise or a spontaneous 'brainstorming'. In either case, the questions should be collected and written on the blackboard.]
There are two main questions:
— What draws the children to the chest?
— Where do they disappear to?
In addition, the narrative fails to satisfy the reader's curiosity on the following points, which may or may not be relevant:
— Why do the children come to live with their grandmother? (**13** 1–2)
— What has happened to their parents? (**13** 16–17, **14** 8–9)
— Why does the old lady need to be introduced to her grandchildren?
— Is she really being kind to the children? (**13** 10–18, etc.)
— Who are "Ann" and "Mrs Fenn"? (**13** 14–15)
— What does the grandmother know? (**14** 16, 26–28)
— Does she really want the children to avoid the chest? (**14** 27–28)

Homework: Re-read the story, to try to find — or guess — the answers to some of these questions.

Unit II
The Riddle: Possible Explanations

In our experience, this story gives rise to widely varying reactions and interpretations. We therefore strongly advise against imposing any one reading of this piece of fiction on the class as being in any way definitive. The following unit includes two different approaches to the story. We recommend that one approach (A or B) be concentrated on, with a brief reference to the alternative view. For weaker classes, the more straightforward and less speculative version A is to be preferred. To deal in full with *both* alternative interpretations would call for a third teaching unit, which is only recommended for advanced students.

General discussion:
Did you understand the story better on reading it the second time?
Were you able to answer any of the open questions?
Which of the questions do you think are important?

[The latter point should give an indication whether the pupils tend to see the human feelings, behaviour and relationships as more important, with the 'supernatural' elements as being in some way allegorical (sequence A), or to see it as a story of the supernatural, in which human motivation is not very relevant (sequence B).]

A. A transformation of the 'cautionary tale'

1. *Could you describe the fate of the children as a kind of punishment?*
In going near the oak chest, the children are obviously disobeying their grandmother's order (**13** 18–22; **14** 16–18, 27–28). So their disappearance can be said to be their own fault, and a warning to other children to ignore such orders at their peril.

2. *What makes this story different from other 'cautionary tales' you may know?*
An obvious comparison would be with the well-known *Struwwelpeter*. In most genuine 'cautionary tales', the children who are punished have been seen to do something bad: one is not meant to feel sorry for them, or sympathize with them until they have learned the error of their ways. But here, one cannot help sympathizing with the children right from the start.

3. *Are the children happy in their new home? Consider the way each of them is drawn to the oak chest.*
We are told that the children do indeed begin to feel at home in the old house (**13** 25–27). There is a reference to them going to school (**13** 17), which indicates that their normal life continues uninterrrupted. But one still gets the impression that they are shut away from the real world in the gloomy old house. The children are never found playing in the open, e.g. under the "elm tree" (**13** 5) or in the "green fields" behind the house (**14** 33).
In this claustrophobic situation, the children's interest in the chest seems to lie within the scope of their natural curiosity. But in addition, their playing with the forbidden chest is evidently a means of compensating for the things they clearly miss in the old lady's home. So the chest evokes Henry's longing for motherly warmth and nearness (**14** 8–10), Matilda's quest for company (**14** 19–24), Harriet's and William's romanticism or emerging sexuality (**14** 38–**15**, 3), James's and Dorothea's thirst for uncommon adventures (**15** 8–14), and finally Ann's unappeased hunger for fantastic worlds (**15** 25–37). Tellingly enough, several references to the oak chest coincide with references to the window of this strange bedroom which separates this restricted world from the real world outside (**13** 19–20; **14** 7–8, 33; **15** 35).

4. *Considering the children's needs, how appropriate do you consider the old lady's attitude to them?*
If compared with the children's spontaneity, curiosity and needs, the old lady's 'kindness' seems to be repressive. Two distinct principles oppose each other in this old Georgian house. At the one end, there is this formal ceremonious kindness which allows no variation (**13** 11, 15–16, 21–22, 30–31; **14** 11–12; **15** 15–16) and selfishly demands "smiling faces" (**13** 13–17) whether there is a reason for smiles or not. The old lady's mental immobility is quite striking. Something about the chest in the bedroom seems to prevent her from taking a genuine interest in the children's games and their tragic ends (e.g. **14** 13–18). The subsequent loss of her grandchildren is accepted as a matter of course (cf. **14** 16, **15** 20–22), and with a touch of self-pity rather than with any feelings of real regret. With a view to what has happened, the comfort she administers to the children sounds banal (**14** 16–26). She seems to be losing touch with reality, and can be said to be living in the past (**13** 23–24, 29–30; **16** 9–12).

Suggested blackboard notes at the end of this sequence:

conflicting forces	*children's needs*
formality ↔ spontaneity	warmth
immobility ↔ vitality	tenderness
indifference ↔ longing	companionship
age ↔ youth	adventures
the past ↔ the present	...
death ↔ life	

5. *Which side do you think the author is on?*
He is obviously on the side of the children, and their real human needs. The grandmother is at best a pathetic figure, and at worst a sinister one. So instead of supporting the authority of social conventions, as in the usual 'cautionary tale', the author can be said to be undermining it.

B. An unusual 'ghost story'

1. *What clues are given in the story about the family background of the children, and the reason why they came to live with their grandmother?*
13 16–17: The old lady's "own son Harry" must be the children's father, now dead. The children's mother must also be dead (**14** 8–9), which would explain why they came to live with their grandmother. (Were the parents killed in an accident? Murdered?)

13 9–10: It seems strange that a grandmother would need to be introduced to her orphaned grandchildren. Either the family had lived very far away (in the colonies?) or the parents were estranged from the old lady. Note that the old lady wants to be reminded of her son as a child, and not as a grown man: maybe she objected to his marriage?

2. *The main question of the story is, what has happened to the children? Can there be a natural explanation?*
There is no natural explanation for their disappearance, and it is difficult to explain this away in terms of allegory or illusions. It really seems as if the children are being spirited away by some force which manifests itself in the old chest. The supernatural nature of what is drawing them to the chest is most evident in the case of the first and last children to disappear, Henry and Ann.

3. *What might their familiy history have to do with their disappearance?*
If the children's parents were really estranged from the old lady, they might not feel happy about them living with her in the old house. In any case, since they are dead, they can (at least in the conventions of the ghost story) make their presence felt as spirits. A violent death is supposed to make this more likely.
There is one suggestion in the story of a link between the mysterious old chest and the children's mother (**14** 8–9). Maybe it is her spirit which is drawing them to the chest, drawing them to join her in the world of spirits?

4. *What is the grandmother's role in this 'ghost story'?*
Why do you think she is so indifferent to the fate of the children?
She remains a very mysterious figure. She seems to have a foot in both worlds, as it were: still alive and resident in a solid Georgian house somewhere in England, but very old and feeble and fast losing contact with reality (**13** 23–24, **15** 6–7). Her daydreams about the past (**13** 16–17, 29–30; **16** 9–12) may well be turning into a longing for death, when she might hope to be reunited with her old friends and especially her son Harry. Such a view of life would tally with her apparent indifference to the disappearance of the children, and the half-heartedness of her warnings.

Can you explain her lack of surprise at the children's disappearance?
Her lack of surprise must be linked with the inside knowledge she seems to have about the powers of the old chest (**13** 19–22, **14** 26–28, etc.). Whether she has always known of its supernatural powers, or whether it is her closeness to death which is putting her in contact with the world of spirits, is a matter for speculation.

5. *No 'ghosts' are actually seen in this story. What is it that gives it such a ghostly atmosphere?*

Apart from the strange happenings, a number of details add up to a very ghostly atmosphere:

— Ghosts can, of course, appear anywhere, but are commonly believed to prefer old houses. The description of this one (see Unit I, point 2) makes it seem a very strange place. One gets the impression that it isolates its inhabitants from the real world of green fields and busy streets outside, and brings them closer to this 'other' world.

— A ghostly atmosphere is conjured up by repeated references to darkness or faint light: "evening twilight", "dark smiling heads", "glimmering white dress", "dusk", "looked out between the candles" (all **13** 32–**14** 15; see also **15** 34–41, **16** 6–9). The references to quietness (e.g. **14** 32) and sweet smells (e.g. **14** 23) have a similar effect.

— The story is full of references to past memories, dreams, day-dreams, fantasy, make-believe and fiction, all of which are made to seem as 'real' as the reality of the outside world — or even more real, as the latter fades from view (cf. esp. **13** 23–24 and **15** 32). In each case, some such memory, fantasy or piece of make-believe is instrumental in transporting the children out of this world via the mysterious chest. The same seems to be true of the old lady as she approaches death.

Ray Bradbury

A Piece of Wood

"Sit down, young man," said the Official.

"Thanks." The young man sat.

"I've been hearing rumors about you," the Official said pleasantly. "Oh, nothing much. Your nervousness. Your not getting on so well. Several months now I've heard about you, and I thought I'd call you in. Thought maybe you'd like your job changed. Like to go overseas, work in some other War Area? Desk job killing you off, like to get right in on the old fight?"

"I don't think so," said the young sergeant.

"What *do* you want?"

The sergeant shrugged and looked at his hands. "To live in peace. To learn that during the night, somehow, the guns of the world had rusted, the bacteria had turned sterile in their bomb casings, the tanks had sunk like prehistoric monsters into roads suddenly made tar pits. That's what I'd like."

"That's what we'd all like, of course," said the Official. "Now stop all that idealistic chatter and tell me where you'd like to be sent. You have your choice – the Western or the Northern War Zone." The Official tapped a pink map on his desk.

But the sergeant was talking at his hands, turning them over, looking at the fingers: "What would you officers do, what would we men do, what would the *world* do if we all woke tomorrow with the guns in flaking ruin?"

The Official saw that he would have to deal carefully with the sergeant. He smiled quietly. "That's an interesting question. I like to talk about such theories, and my answer is that there'd be mass panic. Each nation would think itself the only unarmed nation in the world, and would blame its enemies for the disaster. There'd be waves of suicide, stocks collapsing, a million tragedies."

"But *after* that," the sergeant said. "After they realized it was true, that every nation was disarmed and there was nothing more to fear, if we were all clean to start over fresh and new, what then?"

"They'd rearm as swiftly as possible."

"What if they could be stopped?"

"Then they'd beat each other with their fists. If it got down to that. Huge armies of men with boxing gloves of steel spikes would gather at the national borders. And if you took the gloves away they'd use their finger-nails and feet. And if you cut their legs off they'd *spit* on each other. And if you cut off their tongues and stopped their mouths with corks they'd fill the atmosphere so full of hate that mosquitoes would drop to the ground and birds would fall dead from telephone wires."

"Then you don't think it would do any good?" the sergeant said.

"Certainly not. It'd be like ripping the carapace off a turtle. Civilization would gasp and die from the shock."

The young man shook his head. "Or are you lying to yourself and me because you've a nice comfortable job?"

"Let's call it ninety per cent cynicism, ten per cent rationalizing the situation. Go put your Rust away and forget about it."

The sergeant jerked his head up. "How'd you know I *had* it?" he said.

"Had what?"

"The Rust, of course."

"What're you talking about?"

"I *can* do it, you know. I could start the Rust tonight if I wanted to."

The Official laughed. "You can't be serious."

"I am. I've been meaning to come talk to you. I'm glad you called me in. I've worked on this invention for a long time. It's been a dream of mine. It has to do with the structure of certain atoms. If you study them you find that the arrangement of atoms in steel armor is such-and-such an arrangement. I was looking for an imbalance factor. I majored in physics and metallurgy, you know. It came to me, there's a Rust factor in the air all the time. Water vapor. I had to find a way to give steel a 'nervous breakdown.' Then the water vapor everywhere in the world would take over. Not on all metal, of course. Our civilization is built on steel, I wouldn't want to destroy most buildings. I'd just eliminate guns and shells, tanks, planes, battleships. I can set the machine to work on copper and brass and aluminum, too, if necess-ary. I'd just walk by all of those weapons and just being near them I'd make them fall away."

The Official was bending over his desk, staring at the sergeant. "May I ask you a question?"

"Yes."

"Have you ever thought you were Christ?"

"I can't say that I have. But I have considered that God was good to me to let me find what I was looking for, if that's what you mean."

The Official reached into his breast pocket and drew out an expensive ball-point pen capped with a rifle shell. He flourished the pen and started filling in a form. "I want you to take this to Dr Mathews this afternoon, for a complete check-up. Not that I expect anything really bad, understand. But don't you feel you *should* see a doctor?"

"You think I'm lying about my machine," said the sergeant. "I'm not. It's so small it can be hidden in this cigarette package. The effect of it extends for nine hundred miles. I could tour this country in a few days, with the machine set to a certain type of steel. The other nations couldn't take advantage of us because I'd rust their weapons as they approach us. Then I'd fly to Europe. By this time next month the world would be free of war forever. I don't know how I found this invention. It's impossible. Just as impossible as the atom bomb. I've waited a month now, trying to think it over. I worried about what would happen if I did rip off the carapace, as you say. But now I've just about decided. My talk with you has helped clarify things. Nobody thought an aeroplane would ever fly, nobody thought an atom would ever explode, and nobody thinks that there can ever be Peace, but there *will* be."

"Take that paper over to Dr Mathews, will you?" said the Official hastily.

The sergeant got up. "You're not going to assign me to any new Zone then?"

"Not right away, no. I've changed my mind. We'll let Mathews decide."

"I've decided then," said the young man. "I'm leaving the Post within the next few minutes. I've a pass. Thank you very much for giving me your valuable time, sir."

"Now look here, Sergeant, don't take things so seriously. You don't have to leave. Nobody's going to hurt you."

"That's right. Because nobody would believe me. Goodbye, sir." The sergeant opened the office door and stepped out.

The door shut and the Official was alone. He stood for a moment looking at the door. He sighed. He rubbed his hands over his face. The phone rang. He answered it abstractedly.

"Oh, *hello*, Doctor. I was just going to call you." A pause. "Yes, I was going to send him over to you. Look, is it all right for that young man to be wandering about? It *is* all right? If you say so, Doctor. Probably needs a rest, a good long one. Poor boy has a delusion of rather an interesting sort. Yes, yes. It's a shame. But that's what a Sixteen-Year War can do to you, I suppose."

The phone voice buzzed in reply.

The Official listened and nodded. "I'll make a note on that. Just a second." He reached for his ball-point pen. "Hold on a moment. Always mislaying things." He patted his pocket. "Had my pen here a moment ago. Wait." He put down the phone and searched his desk, pulling out drawers. He checked his blouse pocket again. He stopped moving. Then his hands twitched slowly into his pocket and probed down. He poked his thumb and forefinger deep and brought out a pinch of something.

He sprinkled it on his desk blotter: a small filtering powder of yellow-red rust.

He sat staring at it for a moment. Then he picked up the phone. "Mathews," he said, "get off the line, quick." There was a click of someone hanging up and then he dialed another call. "Hello, Guard Station, listen, there's a man coming past you any minute now, you know him, name of Sergeant Hollis, stop him, shoot him down, kill him if necessary, don't ask any questions, kill the son of a bitch, you heard me, this is the Official talking! Yes, kill him, you hear!"

"But, sir," said a bewildered voice on the other end of the line. "I can't, I just *can't* . . ."

"What do you mean you can't, God damn it!"

"Because . . ." The voice faded away. You could hear the guard breathing into the phone a mile away.

The Official shook the phone. "Listen to me, listen, get your gun ready!"

"I can't shoot anyone," said the guard.

The Official sank back in his chair. He sat blinking for half a minute, gasping.

Out there even now – he didn't have to look, no one had to tell him – the hangars were dusting down in soft red rust, and the aeroplanes were blowing away on a brownrust wind into nothingness, and the tanks were sinking, sinking slowly into the hot asphalt roads, like dinosaurs (isn't that what the man had said?) sinking into primordial tar pits. Trucks were blowing away into ochre puffs of smoke, their drivers dumped by the road, with only the tires left running on the highways.

"Sir . . ." said the guard, who was seeing all this, far away. "Oh, God . . ."

"Listen, listen!" screamed the Official. "Go after him, get him, with your hands, choke him, with your fists, beat him, use your feet, kick his ribs in, kick him to death, do anything, but get that man. I'll be right out!" He hung up the phone.

By instinct he jerked open the bottom desk drawer to get his service pistol. A pile of brown rust filled the new leather holster. He swore and leaped up.

On the way out of the office he grabbed a chair. It's wood, he thought. Good old-fashioned wood, good old-fashioned maple. He hurled it against the wall twice, and it broke. Then he seized one of the legs, clenched it hard in his fist, his face bursting red, the breath snorting in his nostrils, his mouth wide. He struck the palm of his hand with the leg of the chair, testing it. "All right, God damn it, come on!" he cried.

He rushed out, yelling, and slammed the door.

Biographical Notes

Ray Bradbury was born in Illinois, in 1920. While still at High School, he began to write stories of fantasy, reflecting his childhood interest in circuses, magicians, thought readers, etc., and his avid consumption of sensational literature and comics. After leaving school he continued to write, earning his living on the side as a newspaper vendor.

On his twenty-first birthday he was surprised by the publication of one of his stories in a popular magazine. Soon his stories began appearing in quality magazines, and several were included in the annual anthologies Best American Short Stories. *His most successful works are the sequence of short stories published as* The Martian Chronicles *(1950), and the novel* Fahrenheit 451 *(1951). The latter was turned into a film (directed by François Truffaut) in 1966.*

In almost all of his stories, Ray Bradbury can be said to use the form of science fiction as a vehicle for reflection about present tendencies.

Annotations

19 13 **casing** protective metallic covering – 17 **chatter** *(n.)* foolish talk – 22 **flaking** with bits falling off the surface – 27 **suicide** ['su:ɪsaɪd] act of killing oneself – **stocks collapsing** shares in a company (Aktien) losing their value – 32 **swift** quick, fast

20 9 **to rip off** to remove s.th. quickly and violently – **carapace** ['kærəpeɪs] hard shell on the back of certain animals – **turtle** Schildkröte – 13 **to rationalize** to find reasonable-sounding explanations for – 15 **to jerk** to make a short, quick movement – 24 **armo(u)r** ['ɑ:mə] strong protective covering – 25 **to major in** *Am.* to study as a main subject – 27 **vapo(u)r** ['veɪpə] gas, steam – 30 **to eliminate** to do away with – **shell** metal case filled with explosives – 31 **brass** hard yellow metal made by mixing copper and zinc

21 2 **to flourish** ['flʌrɪʃ] to wave in a showy manner – 7 **to extend** to reach – 20 **to assign** [ə'saɪn] to give a particular job or position to s.o. – 23 **the Post** *here:* the military camp – 32 **abstractedly** lost in thought – 36 **delusion** false belief

22 3 **to mislay** to lose – 6 **to twitch** to make short, sharp movements – **to probe** to search – **to poke** to push into – 7 **pinch** very small amount of s.th. (Prise) – 8 **blotter** piece of thick soft paper for drying ink – 15 **son of a bitch** *Am. vulg.* term of abuse, like 'bastard' – 17 **bewildered** [bɪ'wɪldəd] confused, puzzled – 24 **to blink** (of eyes) to open and shut quickly – 27 **hangar** building in which aeroplanes are kept – 30 **primordial** [praɪ'mɔ:dɪəl] existing from the earliest times – 31 **ochre** ['əʊkə] brownish-yellow – 35 **to choke** to stop s.o. breathing – 39 **to swear** ['sweə] **swore, sworn** to express one's anger through the use of vulgar language

23 2 **maple** [eɪ] type of northern tree with pointed leaves (Ahorn) – **to hurl** to throw with great force – 3 **to seize** [i:] to take hold of – **to clench** to hold firmly – 4 **to snort** to blow air through one's nose – 7 **to yell** to shout

Interpretation and Teaching Notes

Summary and Analysis

An army official has summoned a young sergeant to his office. Alluding to some rumours about the sergeant's "nervousness", he suggests a transfer to "some other War Area". But the sergeant has his doubts. He would prefer to see all weapons rusted overnight so that he can live in peace.

After the official has made a first attempt to put a stop to what he calls the sergeant's "idealistic chatter" (**19** 17), he is confronted with the (apparently theoretical) question of how people would react to a sudden worldwide destruction of all weapons. The official carefully argues that something like this would only lead to mass panic, with each nation blaming its enemies for the disaster. The official sees himself forced to make a longer statement concerning people's natural disposition to mutual destruction. When he finishes by advising him to "put (his) rust away" (**20** 14) and to forget about the idea, the soldier surprises him with the announcement that he might "start the Rust tonight" (**20** 19).

The sergeant, a former student of physics and metallurgy, claims to have made an invention, a machine the size of a cigarette package, which can make all weapons rust within a range of 900 miles (**21** 10). The sergeant's disclosures, though first met with scorn, begin to alarm the official. He orders the soldier to report immediately to the doctor of the post. But the young man says that he is leaving the post and walks out of the office.

Abstractedly the official answers the doctor's phone call to report about the sergeant's delusion, the effect of "a Sixteen-Year War" (**21** 37), as he thinks. Discovering that his ball-point pen has been turned into yellow rust, he asks the doctor to get off the line. He dials the Station Guard and orders him "to stop, to shoot down and kill" the sergeant if necessary (**22** 14). But the guard retorts ambiguously that he can't shoot anybody. In a shocking vision the official pictures a heap of rusting weapons outside his office. Hysterically he orders the guard "to choke, to beat and kick" the sergeant "to death" (**22** 35).

When he wants to take out his service pistol, the official only finds a pile of brown rust in the holster. Cursing wildly, and with the leg of a smashed chair as a weapon, he rushes out of his office in pursuit of the sergeant.

"A Piece of Wood" (note the pun on the first word) is a science fiction story which reveals the writer's deep distrust of man's technical intelligence[1]. Here, it has combined with human aggression to trap the human race in the no-win situation of eternal warfare — a situation not unlike that in Orwell's *1984*. Conformity and an unquestioning acceptance of the necessity for war seems to be the only way an individual can survive (cf. **20** 11–14). Bradbury does not seem to be too concerned with the technical details of the young man's invention, or with the plausibility of a war dragging on for so long in an age in which nuclear weapons are, at the very least, available (cf. **21** 13). He is more concerned with exploring some theoretical consequences of the unholy alliance between human agression and technology.

Ironically, it takes a technological innovation in the form of the young man's invention to defeat technology. The position with regard to aggression is somewhat similar. In defence of their respective positions, both soldiers resort to the use of force. For the official, a stubborn military executive, there seems to be only one thing that matters: to get rid of this disquieting young trouble-maker as quickly as possible — if necessary, by killing him.

The young man, though he obviously rejects violence as a solution to human conflicts, himself sees no other way of putting an end to violence except by an act of force — a *fait accompli* which deprives the aggressors of their weapons. At the end of the story, military technology does seem to be defeated. Human aggression, however, still remains. The official's own reaction seems to support the view of human nature he expressed earlier in the story (**20** 1–7). But even if this is Bradbury's own view, he at the same time raises the question whether it might not be desirable for such murderous creatures to be deprived of their advanced military technology: with a piece of wood one can do considerably less damage than with an atom bomb.

The way the story is presented allows the reader maximum freedom to speculate on the rights and wrongs of the matter. The neutral 'camera eye' point of view betrays little of the feelings of the two men. (The few deviations towards the official's point of view are minor and can be seen as interpretations of his visible reactions: **18** 23, **22** 26, **23** 1.) Since the dialogue takes up the greater part of the story, this is our main source of information. The reader is, as it were, put in the position of a listener who may take note of what is being said, may probe the speakers' logic and in the end arrive at some interesting conclusions concerning the nature of human aggression and its consequences for the future of the human race.

1 cf. Eike Barmeyer, *Science Fiction. Theorie und Geschichte.*
(UTB) München, 1972, p. 125

Unit I
Setting, Structure, Characters

Preparatory work: Read the whole story. Then pick out all details that refer to the setting of the story.

1. The setting

Where and when does the story take place?

Bradbury's story is set in the office of a fictitious military post (**19** 1, 7, 9, 19; **21** 23) located somewhere outside Europe in an indeterminate 'future' (**21** 10–11). The telephone conversation between the official and the doctor reveals that this post is part of a war which has been going on for sixteen years (**21** 37). Military thinking had divided the world into various "War Zones" (**19** 6–7, 18). Moreover, the soldiers' discussion gives the reader some insight into the arsenal of this conflict: ordinary rifles, bacteria, bombs, tanks, aeroplanes, battleships as well as nuclear weapons (**19** 12–13, **20** 30, **21** 13, 16). This common triad of conventional, bacteriological and nuclear weapons leaves us with the impression that this World War is not so terribly far away from our time.

2. The structure of the narrative

How many parts would you divide the story into? Suggest headlines for each section.

[It would be advisable to first discuss the possible criteria for dividing up the story, and then allow the students a silent phase to re-read it.]

— One simple approach might be to follow Bradbury's division into 'scenes' through the entry or exit of characters. Accordingly, this would lead to a division of the story into four sections:
  19 1–**21** 29: the official's discussion with the sergeant in the office;
  21 30–**22** 11: the official's telephone talk with the doctor;
  22 11–**22** 37: the official's telephone call to the Guard Station;
  22 38–**23** 7: the official's rush from the office.

— Another (more profitable) approach would be to follow the easily discernible changes in the official's mood, with which his final eruption is prepared:
  19 1–**19** 19: elaborate politeness mixed with patronization;
  19 20–**20** 14: serious argumentation which turns emotional;
  20 15–**21** 30: growing unease and alarm;
  21 31–**22** 37: consternation and panic;
  22 38–**23** 7: violent action.
  [This approach is further developed in point 3.]

— A third, more sophisticated approach would be to work oneself along the idea "rust" which keeps running through the whole story as a leitmotif. The essential facts of the action would then have to be built round this key word and its connotations (**19** 12; **20** 14, 19, 26; **21** 10, **22** 8–9, 27, 28, 39; for indirect references see **19** 22, **20** 32–33). This would justify three main divisions:
19 1–**20** 14: wishful thinking
20 15–**21** 40: real potential
22 1–**23** 7: rust in action

3. The characters
How do the official's changing moods relate to his view of the sergeant?
[The students' answers should lead to the following blackboard sketch:]

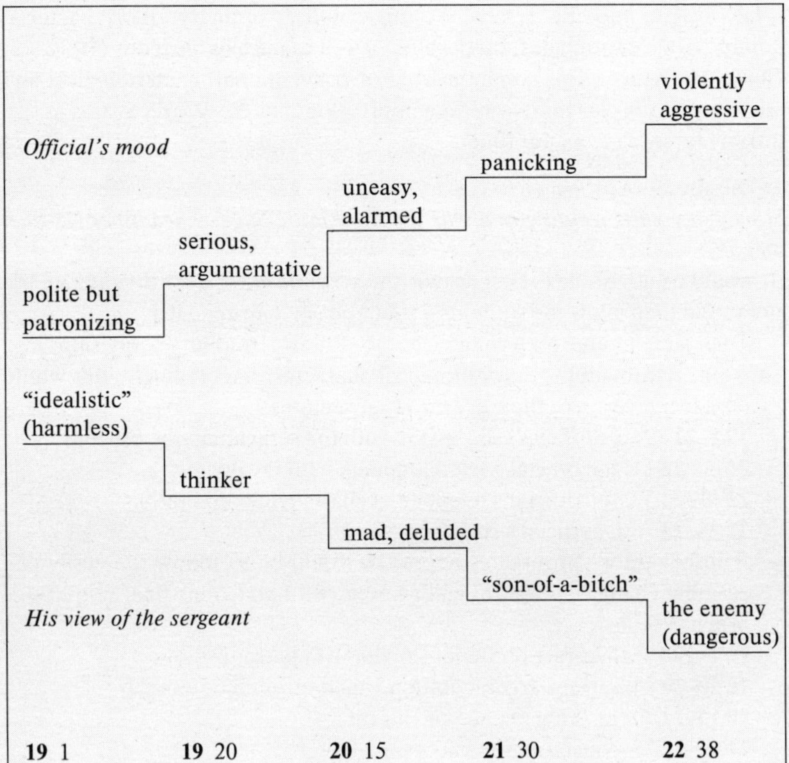

Is the official's view of the young man correct? Explain what impression you get of both men — and why.
The official's reactions to the sergeant (see above) tell us more about himself than about the young man.
He may be characterized as a conformist and typical bureaucrat. The confrontation with the young man clearly shows his intellectual and social shortcomings. His arguments are intelligent, but it is clear (**19** 23–24) that he is putting on an act for the young man's benefit. He first seems to take cover behind a barricade of joviality, and then one of scorn and dogmatism. These protective barriers break down, or are abandoned, when the official finds himself in an unprecedented situation: the apparent breakdown of the ordered military world in which he had felt secure (cf. **20** 11–14).

The young man seems to be a genuine idealist, but one who could also be characterized — depending on one's view of such people — as an eccentric or political fanatic. His emotional involvement can be seen in the nervous gestures which accompany his words at the beginning of the conversation (**19** 11, 21–22). But this does not cloud his reasoning, which is at least as logical as the official's. The young man's conviction that "there *will* be" peace once all weaponry is turned to rust, reveals his main weakness: an exaggerated optimism which does not take human nature into account. Unlike the official, however, he is fully sincere, and is using this talk with the official as a means of clarifying his own ideas and intentions (cf. **19** 20–22, **20** 21, **21** 23–25).

4. Narrative technique [This point may be omitted, since it is dealt with in detail in connection with the next story.]
How do you get to know what the characters are like?
Our judgement of both characters is based mainly on what we hear them say. There are a couple of minor 'interpretations' of what the official is thinking (**19** 23, **22** 26, **23** 1), but the overall point of view is that of a neutral (invisible) observer, or 'camera eye'.

Homework: a) Re-read the story to prepare a discussion on the validity of the arguments presented in it. [For all students.]
b) Try to produce a tape-recording with one of your friends of the official's talk with the sergeant, **19** 1–**21** 28. [Optional extra.]

Unit II
The Central Conflict

1. War and human nature

Comment on the official's and the sergeant's attitudes towards war.

The official regards war as inevitable, whereas the young sergeant sees it as a scourge of mankind which it should be possible to do away with. To all appearances, this conflict is based on the two soldiers' different notions of human nature.

The official's opinion is based on the assumption that man is an extremely distrustful and aggressive being (**19** 25–28; **20** 1–7). For this reason, organized and armed warfare is absolutely necessary in order to maintain the nations' welfare (**19** 25–28); indeed it is vital to human civilization (**20** 9–10). The absurdity involved here — that this civilization involves mutual annihilation with ever increasing efficiency — is something the official obviously prefers not to think about. He turns a deaf ear to the young man's objections, but admits that he is, in part, just "rationalizing the situation" (**20** 13–14).

[This pessimistic view of man's nature is a distorted echo of the philosophy of Thomas Hobbes. In *Leviathan*, he presents a very negative picture of the state of nature before it is tamed by the establishment of an allpowerful state: "bellum ominium contra omnes", "homo homini lupus". Extracts — or a summary — could be read to the class, for comparison.]

By contrast, there is the sergeant's unshakable belief that people are, in principle, capable of peace once disarmament is forced on them through a *fait accompli*. He does not say what his optimism is based on, except to hint at the universal *desire* for peace (**19** 11, **21** 11, 17). If he is right, and man is basically peaceful, then it is difficult to explain the fact of war. By the hopes he puts on a fresh start (**19** 29–31), he seems to be implying that somewhere in the course of history man has gone astray, and that this can be put right.

Which view of human nature do you think is correct?

How would you explain the existence of war and aggression?

[Personal opinions are called for here. Starting from an analysis of the contradictions involved in both the extreme views, the students could try to formulate alternative, and more plausible explanations for the prevalence of warfare.]

2. Technology and warfare

How do the two characters see the role of technology?

The official represents the view that seems to be dominant in his society, as it is in ours — i.e. the view that technology is essential to modern civilization. The fact that it is used for mutual destruction does not cause him to question its value. Rather, he tries to justify this by postulating a psychological need for sophisticated military defences.

In his desire for peace, the young man fixed his attention on the role of technology. He occasionally seems to regard it as the *cause* of war (**19** 11–15), and thinks its elimination would therefore be the solution — that it would at least give mankind a chance to 'start anew'. Note that he does not reject all of technology, however (**20** 28–30), merely that part of it which human beings use for their mutual destruction. And tellingly, it is with a technological innovation of his own with which he hopes to 'save the world'.

Do you think the author is siding with any one view?

Bradbury's story paints a dismal picture of future times. He certainly cannot be identifying with the official's unquestioning and somewhat cynical acceptance of a patently absurd situation. In making the young man the more likeable of the two characters, he seems to be suggesting sympathy for such views. [This is the case in a number of other Bradbury stories as well, where characters express such opinions as "Science ran too far ahead of us too quickly, and the people got lost in a mechanical wilderness" (from "The Million Year Picnic" in *The Martian Chronicles*, New York 1950; pp. 179–180 Bantam edition); "I ask you, Tom, how did we get in such a state, cities all junk, roads like jigsaws from bombs and half the cornfields glowing with radio-activity at night?" (from "The Smile" in *The Day It Rained Forever*, Penguin Books, Harmondsworth 1963; p. 123).]

3. The ending of the story

What — if anything — is proved by the official's behaviour at the end of the story?

His violent outburst seems to support what he had been saying all along about aggression being part of human nature. This falls short of being proof, since the official may have been conditioned by years as part of an efficient military machine. But there is a strong suggestion that war will go on, with or without technology.

On the other hand, a lot less damage can be done with a "piece of wood" than with sophisticated military technology. So in a sense, the ending of the story suggests that there is some truth in both men's arguments.

Homework: Write an essay of about 200 words, explaining the writer's attitude towards man and technology as shown in this story.

Unit III
The Functions of Fantasy

1. A 'science fiction' story

What kind of a story would you say Bradbury's "A Piece of Wood" is?

The story qualifies as 'science fiction' as it deals with technological developments in an imagined future. The students could look up a dictionary definition of the genre, or a description in a literary encyclopedia, and discuss the various criteria. [A number of alternative definitions are given in *Great Science Fiction Stories: Model Interpretations* (Klett), p. 11.] Such a story can, but does not have to be about science; it can, but does not have to be set in the future. It is always a fantasy of some sort, based on scientific possibilities.

2. Comparison of three different 'fantasies'

What have the first three stories in this book got in common? How do they differ?

All three contain a mixture of the real world, as we know it, and the fantastic, which we have *not* experienced. They differ in the kind of fantasy involved, and in the time settings:

"The Captive Princess"	— imaginary past	— fantasy based on magic powers
"The Riddle"	— imaginary present	— fantasy based on supernatural powers
"A Piece of Wood"	— imaginary future	— fantasy based on scientific possibilities.

3. Functions of fantasy in fairy tales and stories of the supernatural

For what purpose(s) has fantasy been used in "The Captive Princess" and "The Riddle"?

The fairy tale was obviously told with the double aim of entertaining and edifying the (young) listener/reader. De la Mare's intentions are more difficult to pinpoint, but both elements are also present. In both cases, the fantastic elements are entertaining, since they free the imagination from the bonds of the 'real' world, and edifying, in that they can influence the reader's/listener's behaviour or way of thinking. They force us to contemplate alternatives to the world we know — or think we know.

[Advanced students could discuss the following quote from Eric S. Rabkin, *Fantastic Worlds: Myths, Tales and Stories*, New York (OUP) 1979, p. 19: "... the fantastic comes not from mere violation of 'the real world', but from offering an alternative to the real world; not from an alternative to some real world of immutable and universal law, but to a real world which our life and education have trained us to project as expectable ...".]

4. The functions of science fiction

In what way is fantasy about scientific possibilities different from fantasy about magic or supernatural powers?

It is more believable in an age when few people believe in fairies or ghosts any more. Science has made so many things possible (cf. **21** 12–17), that it is difficult to rule out any future development, however fantastic.

What has Bradbury's story got to do with the 'real world' as we know it?

The characters are a lot more realistic than in either of the previous stories. The dramatic encounter between the passionate pacifist and inflexible 'brasshat' is quite plausible — easy to imagine in any war situation, past, present or future. The fantastic element — the young man's machine — is more difficult to imagine, but this is not so important. It is the writer's way of toying with an interesting idea ("Can wars be done away with once and for all"?), and encouraging his readers to think about the failings of present-day society.

Additional Homework and Discussion (Grammar Revision):

a) Pick out all the conditional sentences used in the story. Explain the effect of the tenses used. How else could these sentences have been phrased? With what effect?

b) Discuss

— what will happen if the young man gets away/if the official catches up with him;
— what would happen in real life if such an invention were to destroy nuclear technology / all military technology;
— what would have happened in the story if the official's (or the young man's) arguments had been more convincing.

Liam O'Flaherty

His First Flight

The young seagull was alone on his ledge. His two brothers and his sister had already flown away the day before. He had been afraid to fly with them. Somehow when he had taken a little run forward to the brink of the ledge and attempted to flap his wings he became afraid. The great expanse of sea stretched down beneath, and it was such a long way down – miles down. He felt certain that his wings would never support him, so he bent his head and ran away back to the little hole under the ledge where he slept at night. Even when each of his brothers and his little sister, whose wings were far shorter than his own, ran to the brink, flapped their wings, and flew away he failed to muster up courage to take that plunge which appeared to him so desperate. His father and mother had come around calling to him shrilly, upbraiding him, threatening to let him starve on his ledge unless he flew away. But for the life of him he could not move.

That was twenty-four hours ago. Since then nobody had come near him. The day before, all day long, he had watched his parents flying about with his brothers and sister, perfecting them in the art of flight, teaching them how to skim the waves and how to dive for fish. He had, in fact, seen his older brother catch his first herring and devour it, standing on a rock, while his parents circled around raising a proud cackle. And all the morning the whole family had walked about on the big plateau midway down the opposite cliff, taunting him with his cowardice.

The sun was now ascending the sky, blazing warmly on his ledge that faced the south. He felt the heat because he had not eaten since the previous nightfall. Then he had found a dried piece of mackerel's tail at the far end of his ledge. Now there was not a single scrap of food left. He had searched every inch, rooting among the rough, dirt-caked straw nest where he and his brothers and sister had been hatched. He even gnawed at the dried pieces of spotted eggshell. It was like eating part of himself. He had then trotted back and forth from one end of the ledge to the other, his grey body the colour of the cliff, his long grey legs stepping daintily, trying to find some means of reaching his parents without having to fly. But on each side of him the ledge ended in a sheer fall of precipice, with the sea beneath. And between him and his parents there was a deep, wide chasm. Surely he could reach them without flying if he could only move northwards along the cliff face? But then on what could he walk? There was no ledge, and he was not a fly. And above him he could see nothing. The precipice was sheer, and the top of it was perhaps farther away than the sea beneath him.

He stepped slowly out to the brink of the ledge, and, standing on one leg with the other leg hidden under his wing, he closed one eye, then the other, and pretended to be falling asleep. Still they took no notice of him. He saw his two brothers and his sister lying on the plateau dozing, with their heads sunk into their necks. His father was preening the feathers on his white back. Only his mother was looking at him. She was standing on a little high hump on the plateau, her white breast thrust forward. Now and again she tore at a piece of fish that lay at her feet, and then scraped each side of her beak on the rock. The sight of the food maddened him. How he loved to tear food that way, scraping his beak now and again to whet it! He uttered a low cackle. His mother cackled too, and looked over at him.

"Ga, ga, ga," he cried, begging her to bring him over some food. "Gaw-ool-ah," she screamed back derisively. But he kept calling plaintively, and after a minute or so he uttered a joyful scream. His mother had picked up a piece of the fish and was flying across to him with it. He leaned out eagerly, tapping the rock with his feet, trying to get nearer to her as she flew across. But when she was just opposite to him, abreast of the ledge, she halted, her legs hanging limp, her wings motionless, the piece of fish in her beak almost within reach of his beak. He waited a moment in surprise, wondering why she did not come nearer, and then, maddened by hunger, he dived at the fish. With a loud scream he fell outwards and downwards into space. His mother had swooped upwards. As he passed beneath her he heard the swish of her wings. Then a monstrous terror seized him and his heart stood still. He could hear nothing. But it only lasted a moment. The next moment he felt his wings spread outwards. The wind rushed against his breast feathers, then under his stomach and against his wings. He could feel the tips of his wings cutting through the air. He was not falling headlong now. He was soaring gradually downwards and outwards. He was no longer afraid. He just felt a bit dizzy. Then he flapped his wings once and he soared upwards. He uttered a joyous scream and flapped them again. He soared higher. He raised his breast and banked against the wind. "Ga, ga, ga. Ga, ga, ga. Gaw-ool-ah." His mother swooped past him, her wings making a loud noise. He answered her with another scream. Then his father flew over him screaming. Then he saw his two brothers and his sister flying around him curveting and banking and soaring and diving.

Then he completely forgot that he had not always been able to fly, and commenced himself to dive and soar and curvet, shrieking shrilly.

He was near the sea now, flying straight over it, facing straight out over the ocean. He saw a vast green sea beneath him, with little ridges moving over it, and he turned his beak sideways and crowed amusedly. His parents and his brothers and sister had landed on this green floor in front of him. They were beckoning to him, calling shrilly. He dropped his legs to stand on the green sea. His legs sank into it. He screamed with fright and attempted to rise again, flapping his wings. But he was tired and weak with hunger and he could not rise, exhausted by the strange exercise. His feet sank into the green sea, and then his belly touched it and he sank no farther. He was floating on it. And around him his family was screaming, praising him, and their beaks were offering him scraps of dog-fish.

He had made his first flight.

Biographical Notes

Liam O'Flaherty was born in 1897 on the main island of the Aran group off the west coast of Ireland. He was the ninth of ten children who all had to be supported on fifteen acres of rocky land. Gaelic was his native language but he soon started to learn English.

At the age of 13 he was educated for the priesthood at two secondary schools on the mainland which were run by the Holy Ghost Fathers. A few years later, however, he decided against becoming a priest and got a scholarship to study Greek and Latin at University College, Dublin.

At the beginning of the First World War he joined the Irish Guards and fought in France. He returned wounded to the Aran Islands in 1917. The following years he spent travelling widely in Europe and America, earning his living as a stoker, a miner, a lumberjack, and a dock labourer. In 1922 he was back in Ireland and fought in the Civil War on the radical Republican side. Fearing arrest, he escaped to London and there started to write.

Liam O'Flaherty caught the public's attention with his vivid description of the revolutionary war in his short novel, The Informer *(1926). This was made into a Hollywood film directed by John Ford (1935). His other novels,* Skerett *(1932) and* Famine *(1937), are generally considered to be even more successful, in literary terms.*

His great narrative talent also showed in numerous tales of country life, collected in the volumes Spring Sowing *(1924),* The Tent *(1926), and* The Mountain Tavern *(1929). O'Flaherty's ability to observe and identify with nature is unequalled among European writers. This aspect of his art comes out very clearly in the story we have chosen.*

Annotations

25 1 **ledge** narrow, flat shelf coming out from a wall or cliff – 3 **brink** edge at the top of a cliff – 4 **expanse** [–'–] large open area – 10 **to muster courage** to overcome one's fear – **plunge** jump downwards, dive – 12 **to upbraid** to scold, to speak angrily to s.o. – 17 **to skim** to move near the surface, barely touching it – 18 **to devour** [dɪ'vaʊə] to eat up quickly and hungrily – 19 **cackle** sound like that made by a hen – 21 **to taunt** [ɔ:] to try to make s.o. angry by laughing at his faults – **cowardice** ['kaʊədɪs] lack of courage – 22

to ascend [–'–] to get higher – **to blaze** to burn brightly – 25 **scrap** small piece – 27 **to hatch** to make a young bird break through the eggshell – **to gnaw** [nɔ:] to keep biting s.th. hard – 30 **daintily** *here:* stiffly and over-anxiously – 32 **sheer** straight down – **precipice** ['presɪpɪs] steep face of rock – 33 **chasm** ['kæzm] very deep hole

26 8 **to doze** to be half asleep – 9 **to preen** to arrange (feathers) with the beak – 11 **to thrust** to push forward – 13 **beak** a bird's hard and horny mouth – 14 **to whet** to sharpen – 17 **derisively** in a mocking way, laughing at s.o.'s foolishness – **plaintively** in a sad way – 21 **abreast of** on a level with – 22 **limp** loose, not stiff – 26 **to swoop** to rush through the air – 31 **headlong** without control – 32 **to soar** to sail through the air – 33 **dizzy** feeling as if everything were turning round – 35 **to bank (against)** to fly with one side higher than the other – 39 **to curvet** [kɜ:'vet] *here:* to keep changing direction

27 2 **to commence** to begin, to start – **to shriek** [i:] to scream – 4 **ridges** *here:* the long, white tops of the waves – 7 **to beckon** to signal to s.o. to come nearer – 10 **exhausted** very tired – 11 **belly** *here:* the underside of an animal's body

Interpretation and Teaching Notes

Summary and Analysis

"His First Flight" is a lyrical narrative, marked by imaginative insight and melodic, near-poetic prose. Its impact depends upon the reader's willingness to accept the parallels between a bird's first flight, and any human child's need to overcome natural fears in exploring the world. Acceptance is furthered by our awareness that animals do have personalities, their behaviour strongly suggesting that we humans have no monopoly of emotions such as love, fear, joy or even parental responsibility. For all we know, this *may* be what a seagull really feels at such a decisive moment of its life, even if the formulation of its 'thoughts' in words is necessarily anthropomorphic.

The "he" of the title is a young male seagull, left alone on a ledge high above the sea after his two brothers and his sister had successfully made their first 'solo' flights, and joined their parents in the outside, adult-seagull world. Despite their example, and the constant prodding, teasing, and threatening of the entire family, he remains on the ledge, terrified at the thought of jumping off. It was "such a long way down — miles down," and "he felt certain that his wings would never support him." The story covers two days, and we first share the young seagull's plight through a flashback (first paragraph), which clarifies why he is where he is. As the second day dawns, he is extremely hungry, and desperately trying to find a way to join his family without taking the awful plunge. But there is no other way off, except, perhaps, by an appeal to his parents' pity. He steps to the edge of the ledge in an attempt to make them believe that he is falling asleep, and will accidentally fall over. This ploy does not work; only his mother watches, and she does nothing. Finally, he simply cries, begging his mother to help him, to bring him some food. This seems to work, and she flies towards him. But at the last moment, she stops just beyond his reach. "Maddened by hunger" he lunges outward, falls, and experiences a moment of terror. His wings do support him, however; he soars, he is no longer afraid, and his family circles around him, praising him. One more brief moment of fear comes when he lands in the sea, but this too is quickly gone, and he has moved from his lonely ledge, his childhood, to the greater — if more threatening — world of the young adult.

This summary of the plot follows the classic pattern of the 'initiation story'. But whereas it is rather easy to identify the 'initiation' theme, it is extremely difficult to capture the mixture of sadness and sympathy and joy that O'Flaherty has developed in three short pages. The story is a positive statement; the young bird soars with joy once the fear is overcome, and the world is a fascinating place. Yet at the same time, we know very well that the fears of the child are not totally irrational and that the first flight and the first landing will not guarantee the success of all others. Perhaps, the sadness is that we know, as the seagull learns, that one cannot stay on the ledge.

Preparatory Steps

If at all possible, a short (about 10-minute) introduction should be fitted in after the last Unit of "A Piece of Wood". A discussion on the following lines might increase the students readiness to appreciate "His First Flight". On the basis of the stories already read, different types of fantasy will have been discussed with regard to the degree of imaginative effort that goes into them, and the different ways writers or storytellers transcend their direct experience. One could go on to point out that in addition, the writers of all these stories had to imagine what people not too different from ourselves might think, feel and do in the rather strange circumstances described. It could be discussed which of these characters they found most (or least) believable, and why. This will amount to saying which characters they could imagine being or meeting in real life. As preparation for the non-human protagonist of the O'Flaherty story, a useful approach is to ask students which creatures they would like to be (or not like to be) if reincarnation were a fact. Birds, deer, lions and other 'higher' animals are likely to be first choices, with spiders and toads among those regarded as less desirable. It will probably emerge from the discussion that our ability to identify with certain animals has to do with our familiarity with them and with our recognition of a certain kinship.

Homework: Read the complete story.

Unit I
Content and Significance

1. Comprehension
What is this story about?
[The basic plot of the story can be summed up in one or two sentences. Then one should ask about any language difficulties, etc.
Optional (after preliminary discussion): Listen to the recording, or re-read the story in class.]

2. Personal reactions
Did you like the story? Why? Or why not?
[It is safe to assume that a teacher who selects a story usually likes the story, and that students know this. So one should take care not to suggest that only 'yes' answers are expected. Another barrier to unbiased judgements (and one which works in the contrary direction) is the degree to which some students (particularly boys) tend to find the seagull's flight 'embarrassing'. Simply said, to admit sympathy for the seagull — the 'crybaby' — is to remind them of their own reactions in similar situations, reactions of which they are ashamed. One can skirt this problem — if it is perceived as one — by asking whether they are 'amused by' or 'can understand' the predicament of the young seagull, rather than talking in terms of identification and sympathy.]

3. Author's intentions
Why do you think this story was told? (Does it matter what life is like for a seagull?)
[The students who might not have been willing to discuss their own 'sentimental' feelings, at least in front of other students, here have an opportunity to talk about the emotional impact of this story in a more objective, less personal way.] A discussion of the possible reactions of different readers to this story could lead to the following points, any of which could have been the author's main concern:
— Sensitivity is to a large degree dependent upon our ability to feel empathy, that is, to imagine another person's feelings and thoughts.
— The ability to imagine what life is like for a seagull can allow us to view the world, and ourselves, from a different perspective.
— We tend to fall into established ways of thinking, and such a story can exercise our imagination.

— Ethocentrism (or the 'egocentrism' of the human race) can lead us to believe that what we do and how we think and feel is unique or special. A story like this can help to counteract this tendency. (There is the danger however that it may be imposing human standards on non-human creatures).

4. The 'initiation' theme

What are the parallels with human life in this story of a seagull's first flight?
The situation is comparable with any stage of a young person's life, when he or she has to do something for the first time — walk, go to school alone, learn to swim, speak or perform in public, leave home and earn one's living, etc. — in other words, be 'initiated' into a more adult stage of life. Also similar is the child-rearing aspect, with parents egging children on and rewarding them when they succeed.

How important are such comparisons? Are there any lessons for us humans to be learned from the story?
It would be difficult to find any *specific* moral in the story which could be applied to human life. One could discuss the question of parental attitudes here. It is surprisingly common to find young adults holding very strong views about child-raising theories and, moreover, which of these are 'natural'. Those who tend towards the 'sink-or-swim' schools might have less sympathy for the young seagull — and even wonder why the father didn't simply apply a good webbed foot in the tail feathers. Those of the more child-centred persuasions can equally find the family's behaviour to be crude. But since their methods do result in the young seagull's first euphoric flight, one must admit that they got it just about right, that the adult seagulls' parental instincts served them well. More important than any such moral, however, is the message that our own hopes and fears, the terrors and joys that accompany us on our progress towards adulthood, are more universal than we have probably ever imagined.

[This question can of course be altered to fit the class's familiarity with other initiation stories and any previous discussions of the subject (cf. *Stories of Initiation*, with *Model Interpretations*, Klett). The teacher who wishes to develop the initiation theme further could go straight to the final story in our collection, Katherine Mansfield's "Her First Ball".]

Unit II
Point of View

1. Point of view and its effect

From what point of view (or perspective) do we see the story?

Although the story is narrated in the third person, the perspective is not that of an outside observer, but clearly that of the seagull. We are told what the seagull saw, felt, and experienced, his 'thinking' as it were — and nothing else. There is no reference to his parents' feelings, for example, but only to what the young seagull could see of them and think of them. The only intrusive element is that his 'thoughts' are interpreted and put in words by the author-narrator; this becomes particularly noticeable when he uses a human frame of reference for time and direction (**25** 14, 23). One should not make too much of this, however: "twenty-four hours" can be taken as describing a period of time which *can* be experienced by animals, and "south" as meaning the sunny side. Any use of language for describing an animal's experiences is necessarily artificial.

What effect on the reader does this point of view have?

The strongest effect is our tendency to identify with the seagull. We share his feelings and his fears, and are almost forced to compare them with memories of our own feelings in comparable situations. At the same time, we are observers of his situation, and can judge and interpret his behaviour independently. We realize, for example, that his attempt to make his family think that he is falling off the ledge is a childish (very 'human') ploy, and we also sense what his mother is up to when she approaches the ledge. This additional knowledge does not, however, detract from our sympathy for him, but rather adds to it.

2. Comparison with other stories

Consider the other stories you have read. What point of view is used in each case, and how does it differ from "His First Flight"?

- "The Captive Princess": the storyteller pretends to be all-knowing, is free to comment at will on the deeds, thoughts and feelings of any of the characters, is not restricted in any way by time or place (unrestricted perspective/omniscient author).
- "The Riddle": the author is free, as in "The Captive Princess", to move at will, to see into characters' minds, to observe and comment on actions, etc., but chooses only to present certain things. In other words, the reader feels that the author 'knows something' but is not telling us everything (unrestricted perspective/selective omniscience).

— "A Piece of Wood": most of the action and dialogue is presented as if we were watching the story happen. Occasionally, however, we are allowed to share what a character thinks or feels. For example, we are allowed to see into the official's mind at **9** 23; **22** 26–32; and **23** 1–2. The 'omniscience' elements are so limited, however, that they could be inferences from observations. Were the story to be filmed, the official's thoughts could be represented by facial gestures, etc., or scenes through a window ('camera eye' perspective with some limited omniscience).

3. Alternative techniques applied to "His First Flight"
What differences would result if these perspectives were used in "His First Flight?"
[As point of view does involve abstractions, it might be useful to ask students (or groups of students) to rewrite a paragraph (e.g. the first one) completely, using a different perspective. A comparison of the edited versions should reveal the different effects quite well.]
— With an 'omniscient' point of view, the author might begin by telling us not to worry, that all seagulls eventually fly.
— We might be told the thoughts of the other members of the seagull family. Results: We would know more, but be less inclined to identify with the young seagull. The tension would be less.
— With 'selective' omniscience, the author could have easily switched perspectives, for example, letting us first see how the young seagull felt, and then leaving him and only letting us see what the parents were thinking. We might be forced to take sides.
— A 'camera eye' perspective wouldn't allow us to know what the seagull is feeling. It would be just like a nature show on television with the sound turned off — or maybe just the occasional "ga, ga, ga!" with no interpretation.

4. Comparison with first-person narrator [Optional at this point. Can be deferred until a story with a first-person narrator has been discussed.]
Can you think of a way of telling the story that would make the reader sympathize even more with the young seagull?
We could have the story told *by* the seagull himself, in the first person. It might begin "I was alone on the ledge. My two brothers ...". The problem is that this might strain credibility: we can accept that animals have feelings, and to an extent, thoughts, but not that they can tell us about them. A talking seagull would put the story in the realm of pure fantasy, like some Walt Disney films. This is probably why Liam O'Flaherty did *not* use this technique: what he was after was a credible, realistic effect.

Shirley Jackson

Charles

The day my son Laurie started kindergarten he renounced corduroy overalls with bibs and began wearing blue jeans with a belt. I watched him go off the first morning with the older girl next door, seeing clearly that an era of my life was ended, my sweet-voiced nursery-school tot replaced by a long-trousered, swaggering character who forgot to stop at the corner and wave good-bye to me.

He came home the same way, the front door slamming open, his hat on the floor, and the voice suddenly become raucous, shouting, "Isn't anybody *here*?"

At lunch he spoke insolently to his father, spilled his baby sister's milk, and remarked that his teacher said we were not to take the name of the Lord in vain.

"How *was* school today?" I asked, elaborately casual.

"All right," he said.

"Did you learn anything?" his father asked.

Laurie regarded his father coldly. "I didn't learn nothing," he said.

"Anything," I said. "Didn't learn anything."

"The teacher spanked a boy, though," Laurie said, addressing his bread and butter. "For being fresh," he added, with his mouth full.

"What did he do?" I asked. "Who was it?"

Laurie thought. "It was Charles," he said. "He was fresh. The teacher spanked him and made him stand in a corner. He was awfully fresh."

"What did he do?" I asked again, but Laurie slid off his chair, took a cookie, and left, while his father was still saying, "See here, young man."

The next day Laurie remarked at lunch, as soon as he sat down, "Well, Charles was bad again today." He grinned enormously and said, "Today Charles hit the teacher."

"Good heavens," I said, mindful of the Lord's name. "I suppose he got spanked again?"

"He sure did," Laurie said. "Look up," he said to his father.

"What?" his father said, looking up.

"Look down," Laurie said. "Look at my thumb. Gee, you're dumb." He began to laugh insanely.

"Why did Charles hit the teacher?" I asked quickly.

"Because she tried to make him color with red crayons," Laurie said. "Charles wanted to color with green crayons so he hit the teacher and she spanked him and said nobody play with Charles but everybody did."

The third day – it was Wednesday of the first week – Charles bounced a see-saw on the head of a little girl and made her bleed, and the teacher made him stay inside all during recess. Thursday Charles had to stand in a corner during story-time because he kept pounding his feet on the floor. Friday Charles was deprived of blackboard privileges because he threw chalk.

On Saturday I remarked to my husband, "Do you think kindergarten is too unsettling for Laurie? All this toughness and bad grammar, and this Charles boy sounds like such a bad influence."

"It'll be all right," my husband said reassuringly. "Bound to be people like Charles in the world. Might as well meet them now as later."

On Monday Laurie came home late, full of news. "Charles," he shouted as he came up the hill; I was waiting anxiously on the front steps. "Charles," Laurie yelled all the way up the hill, "Charles was bad again."

"Come right in," I said, as soon as he came close enough. "Lunch is waiting."

"You know what Charles did?" he demanded, following me through the door. "Charles yelled so in school they sent a boy in from first grade to tell the teacher she had to make Charles keep quiet, and so Charles had to stay after school. And so all the children stayed to watch him."

"What did he do?" I asked.

"He just sat there," Laurie said, climbing into his chair at the table. "Hi, Pop, y'old dust mop."

"Charles had to stay after school today," I told my husband. "Everyone stayed with him."

"What does this Charles look like?" my husband asked Laurie. "What's his other name?"

"He's bigger than me," Laurie said. "And he doesn't have any rubbers and he doesn't ever wear a jacket."

Monday night was the first Parent-Teachers meeting, and only the fact that the baby had a cold kept me from going; I wanted passionately to meet Charles' mother. On Tuesday Laurie remarked suddenly, "Our teacher had a friend come to see her in school today."

"Charles's mother?" my husband and I asked simultaneously.

"Naaah," Laurie said scornfully. "It was a man who came and made us do exercises, we had to touch our toes. Look." He climbed down from his chair and squatted down and touched his toes. "Like this," he said. He got solemnly back into his chair and said, picking up his fork, "Charles didn't even *do* exercises."

"That's fine," I said heartily. "Didn't Charles want to do the exercises?"

"Naaah," Laurie said. "Charles was so fresh to the teacher's friend he wasn't *let* do exercises."

"Fresh again," I said.

"He kicked the teacher's friend," Laurie said. "The teacher's friend told Charles to touch his toes like I just did and Charles kicked him."

"What are they going to do about Charles, do you suppose?" Laurie's father asked him.

Laurie shrugged elaborately. "Throw him out of school, I guess," he said.

Wednesday and Thursday were routine; Charles yelled during story hour and hit a boy in the stomach and made him cry. On Friday Charles stayed after school again and so did all the other children.

With the third week of kindergarten Charles was an institution in our family; the baby was being a Charles when he filled his wagon full of mud and pulled it through the kitchen; even my husband, when he caught his elbow in the telephone cord and pulled telephone, ashtray, and a bowl of flowers off the table, said, after the first minute, "Looks like Charles."

During the third and fourth weeks it looked like a reformation in Charles; Laurie reported grimly at lunch on Thursday of the third week, "Charles was so good today the teacher gave him an apple."

"What?" I said, and my husband added warily, "You mean Charles?"

"Charles," Laurie said. "He gave the crayons around and he picked up the books afterward and the teacher said he was her helper."

"What happened?" I asked incredulously.

"He was her helper, that's all," Laurie said, and shrugged.

"Can this be true, about Charles?" I asked my husband that night. "Can something like this happen?"

"Wait and see," my husband said cynically. "When you've got a Charles to deal with, this may mean he's only plotting."

He seemed to be wrong. For over a week Charles was the teacher's helper; each day he handed things out and he picked things up; no one had to stay after school.

"The PTA meeting's next week again," I told my husband one evening. "I'm going to find Charles's mother there."

"Ask her what happened to Charles," my husband said. "I'd like to know."

"I'd like to know myself," I said.

On Friday of that week things were back to normal. "You know what Charles did today?" Laurie demanded at the lunch table, in a voice slightly awed. "He told a little girl to say a word and she said it and the teacher washed her mouth out with soap and Charles laughed."

"What word?" his father asked unwisely, and Laurie said, "I'll have to whisper it to you, it's so bad." He got down off his chair and went around to his father. His father bent his head down and Laurie whispered joyfully. His father's eyes widened.

"Did Charles tell the little girl to say *that*?" he asked respectfully.

"She said it *twice,*" Laurie said. "Charles told her to say it *twice.*"

"What happened to Charles?" my husband asked.

"Nothing," Laurie said. "He was passing out the crayons."

Monday morning Charles abandoned the little girl and said the evil word himself three or four times, getting his mouth washed out with soap each time. He also threw chalk.

My husband came to the door with me that evening as I set out for the PTA meeting. "Invite her over for a cup of tea after the meeting," he said. "I want to get a look at her."

"If only she's there," I said prayerfully.

"She'll be there," my husband said. "I don't see how they could hold a PTA meeting without Charles's mother."

At the meeting I sat restlessly, scanning each comfortable matronly face, trying to determine which one hid the secret of Charles. None of them looked to me haggard enough. No one stood up in the meeting and apologized for the way her son had been acting. No one mentioned Charles.

After the meeting I identified and sought out Laurie's kindergarten teacher. She had a plate with a cup of tea and a piece of chocolate cake; I had a plate with a cup of tea and a piece of marshmallow cake. We maneuvered up to one another cautiously, and smiled.

"I've been so anxious to meet you," I said. "I'm Laurie's mother."

"We're all so interested in Laurie," she said.

"Well, he certainly likes kindergarten," I said. "He talks about it all the time."

"We had a little trouble adjusting, the first week or so," she said primly, "but now he's a fine little helper. With occasional lapses, of course."

"Laurie usually adjusts very quickly," I said. "I suppose this time it's Charles's influence."

"Charles?"

"Yes," I said, laughing, "you must have your hands full in that kindergarten, with Charles."

"Charles?" she said. "We don't have any Charles in the kindergarten."

Biographical Notes

Shirley Jackson was born in 1919 in San Francisco, where she spent most of her early life. She studied at Syracuse University, New York. After graduating with a B.A. degree in 1940, she married a well-known literary critic and settled in Vermont.

Eight years later Shirley Jackson published her first novel, The Road Through The Wall *(1948), and a collection of short stories entitled* The Lottery *(1949). The title story had caused a literary sensation when first published in* The New Yorker. *One of her later stories – a dramatic ghost story – was filmed as* The Haunting.

Most of her best-known stories deal with tragic subjects, or with surprising or even shocking developments in an everyday setting. However, the story in our collection shows that she also had a considerable gift for humour.

Shirley Jackson was mother of two daughters and two sons. She died in 1965.

Annotations

30 1 **kindergarten** *Am.* school for children aged about 5–6 – **to renounce** to give up – **overalls** trousers with the front extending above the waist – 2 **bib** *here:* top part of an apron or overalls – 4 **nursery school** school for children under 5 – **tot** very small child – 5 **to swagger** [æ] to walk in a proud and self-important way – 7 **to slam** to hit or push loudly and with force – 8 **raucous** ['rɔ:kəs] sounding rough and unpleasant or loud and rowdy – 10 **insolent** ['– – –] rude, disrespectful – **to spill** to cause a liquid to run over the side of the container – 11 **to take the name of the Lord in vain** to use God's name in a disrespectful way – 13 **elaborate** [ɪ'læbərət] with great care – **casual** ['kæʒʊəl], *here:* seeming not to care – 18 **to spank** to beat (a child) on the behind – 19 **fresh** *Am. coll.* cheeky, rude (cf. *Ger.* 'frech') – 24 **cookie** *Am.* biscuit – 28 **mindful** *here:* taking care not to use 30 – **sure** *Am. coll.* certainly – 32 **gee** [dʒi:] *Am. sl.* expression of surprise – **dumb** [dʌm] *Am. coll.* stupid (cf. *Ger.* 'dumm') – 33 **insane** mad

31 2 **crayon** ['kreɪɒn] stick of coloured wax – 5 **to bounce** *here:* to cause to move down violently – 6 **see-saw** Wippe – 7 **recess** *Am.* break between classes – 8 **to pound** to strike heavily and noisily – 9 **to deprive of** to take away from – 12 **unsettling** disturbing – **toughness** ['tʌfnəs] hard, violent behaviour – 14 **to reassure** [ˌri:ə'ʃʊə] to comfort – **(there are) bound to be** there must be – 18 **to yell** to shout – 21 **grade** *Am.* form, class, year – 26 **Pop** *Am. coll.* Father, Dad – 32 **rubbers** shoes made of rubber – 35 **passionately** *here:* very much – 38 **simultaneous** at the same time – 39 **scornful** full of contempt, disrespectful – 40 **exercises** *here:* physical training

32 1 **to squat** [ɒ] to sit on one's heels – 2 **solemn** ['– –] serious, earnest – 4 **hearty** with feeling – 12 **to shrug** to raise one's shoulders as an expression of ignorance or indifference – 21 **reformation** improvement – 24 **wary** cautious, very careful – 27 **incredulous** [ɪŋ'kredjʊləs] unable to believe – 32 **to plot** to make secret plans – 36 **PTA** Parent-Teacher Association

33 3 **to awe** [ɔ:] to fill with respect – 13 **to abandon** [–'– –] to give up – **evil** ['i:vəl] very bad, wicked – 19 **prayerful** like a prayer – 22 **to scan** to look at closely – **matronly** ['meɪtrənlɪ] (of a woman) middle-aged – 24 **haggard** tired from suffering of anxiety – 29 **marshmallow** soft, spongy sweet – 30 **cautious** ['kɔ:ʃəs] careful – 31 **to be anxious to do s.th.** to have a strong wish to do s.th. – 35 **to adjust** to get used to (new circumstances) – **prim** stiff and self-controlled – 36 **lapse** a fall back into bad habits

Interpretation and Teaching Notes

Summary and Analysis

Little Laurie, who has just started kindergarten, keeps his parents in suspense with more or less shocking stories about his fellow-pupil Charles, who harasses his teacher and classmates with his aggressive behaviour. Charles, for instance, hits the teacher, keeps pounding his feet on the floor during storytime, or yells in class during story hour. Punishment obviously has little effect on him. Fearing that "all this toughness" may have a "bad influence" (**31** 12–13) on Laurie, his mother "passionately" wishes to contact Charles' mother at the first Parent-Teachers meeting (**31** 34–36), but her plan comes to nothing because her baby's cold keeps her from going. Eventually, Laurie's daily reports about Charles begin to dominate both parents' consciousness. By the third week of kindergarten "Charles" has become a synonym for any kind of mischief or damage done within the family (**32** 16–20). After what seems a time of reformation in Charles when his teacher calls him her "helper" (**32** 34), Charles reverts to his usual misbehaviour. Among other things, he makes a little girl say an evil word (**33** 3) and later says it himself "three or four times" (**33** 14). Anxiously, Laurie's mother attends the second Parent-Teachers meeting where no one, however, mentions Charles. When she approaches the teacher after the meeting and introduces herself as Laurie's mother, she is informed primly that her little son had "a little trouble adjusting, the first week or so" (**33** 35), but now has become "a fine little helper. With occasional lapses, of course". Innocently Laurie's mother tries to attribute her son's lapses to "Charles' influence", but the teacher informs her that they "don't have any Charles in the kindergarten". It is only at this point that she realizes that Laurie — give or take an exaggeration or two — has been describing his own behaviour at school. One can only imagine her shock on realizing that she herself is "Charles' mother".

The action of the story covers a time span of a little more than four weeks. (References to chronology: **30** 25; **31** 5,9,11; **32** 13,14,16,17,21,22; **33** 1, 13.) The story is told by the mother, as first-person narrator. She is both observer of the action and closely involved in it. Her feelings, thoughts and reactions during these four weeks are related directly with no trace of hindsight. Consequently, at no point is the truthfulness of Laurie's reports about Charles called into question. For both parents Charles is a 'real' figure; up to the denouement his existence is felt as a constant menace to their little son.

Psychologically speaking, Laurie's daily performances might be seen as an intelligent form of sublimation: for quite a while Laurie successfully transforms his difficulties in adjusting to the social demands of kindergarten life into material for his fight for recognition at home. The reasons for his failure to "adjust" can only be speculated on. The first paragraph suggests that Laurie had acquired certain notions of 'grown-upness' and independence (presumably nurtured by his loving parents) which inevitably clashed with the mild forms of school discipline usual even at the kindergarten stage.

Seen from the reader's perspective, the story makes pleasant reading, because Laurie's tactics will soon be seen through. While the narrator in the story is blind to what is really going on, the reader step by step becomes aware of the improbability of Laurie's reports. The point at which one realises that Laurie is tricking his parents will, of course, vary; but from then on one knows — or suspects — more than the narrator (dramatic irony) and is amused at her expense.

The suspense lies in the question: "How long can Laurie go on tricking his parents?" Consequently, the twist at the end of the story comes as some sort of confirmation rather than as a surprise. The blow is dealt to Laurie's mother, not to the reader. For the juvenile reader, the charm of this story probably lies in a humorous reversal of traditional roles: Parents, by convention thought to be intellectually superior to their children are outwitted by the imagination and artistry of a clever little nipper.

Unit I
The Contents

Preparation: The students should have read the whole story at home, at least in a cursory fashion.

1. Central character and narrator

Who do you think is the main character in the story? Give reasons why.

[Since the father and the schoolteacher will be dismissed as relatively minor characters, and "Charles" as non-existent (at least as a separate individual), one is left with Laurie and his mother — in the order they are likely to be mentioned.]

Laurie: Everybody's attention is centred on him in this story. Even Charles owes his impressive naughtiness to Laurie's imaginative and dramatic talents. All information which concerns Charles comes from one source. It is Laurie's daily reports that make this fictitious character gradually take on contours. Laurie's creation is apparently so convincing that it becomes an instrument in Laurie's hands with which he succeeds in manipulating his parents' feelings. The choice of "Charles" for a title therefore does not contradict Laurie's central position in the story.
Laurie's mother: If not mentioned by any of the students, the teacher should raise the question of her position in the story. Not only is the story told from the mother's point of view, but in her own words, i.e. she is first-person narrator. We have direct access to her thoughts and feelings. However, all we learn about her is that her whole consciousness is — at least for the moment — centred on her little son.

2. Comprehension questions (plot)
What changes does Laurie's mother observe in her son the day he starts kindergarten?
What does Laurie report about Charles in the following two weeks?
How do Laurie's parents respond to these reports?
How does Charles influence life in Laurie's family?
In what way does Charles' conduct change during the third and fourth week?
How do Laurie's parents interpret this change?
How does Charles behave shortly before the second PTA meeting?
What course does the second PTA meeting take for Laurie's mother?
[At this point the story should be read in class for more detailed comprehension — or the recording listened to.]

3. Group work – either as alternative to comprehension questions (above), or as additional assignments.

Group A: *Have a second close reading of the story. – Note down in brief, following the chronological order, all the information you get about Charles' behaviour and about his teacher's corresponding reactions. Enter your findings into a chart, as follows:*

time		Charles	teacher
week	day		
1st	Monday Tuesday	was fresh hit the teacher	spanked Charles spanked Charles again [etc.]

Group B: *Work through the text and note down all relevant information on Laurie's behaviour in outline form (entering the details into a similar chart, if desired).*

First Week:

— Laurie starts wearing blue jeans.

— He goes off to kindergarten without waving goodbye.

— On returning, he shouts and slams the door. [etc.]

Group C: *Summarize the corresponding reactions of Laurie's parents (entering the details into a similar chart, if desired).*

— Laurie's mother notices that an era of her life has come to an end.

— She tries to react casually.

— Laurie's father asks what he learned at school. [etc.]

[This group work should lead to written results available to all students. The tasks of the groups B and C can be combined and allocated to a more advanced group. Part or all of these tasks can be set as written homework.]

Homework: a) Re-read the story for discussion in detail. b) Finish your charts.

Unit II
Humour and Irony

1. Charles' identity

Who is Charles? — How do you know?

[If there is any doubt on the matter, the teacher should ask the pupils use their charts to compare Laurie's behaviour at home with Charles' conduct in the kindergarten. The pupils will then see that from the outset the story contains a number of clues which signal that Charles is more or less identical with Laurie himself.]

Laurie's reports about Charles correspond quite closely with what we see of his behaviour at home. Thus, Laurie's insolence towards his father when he returns from kindergarten (**30** 10–24) is in line with his characterization of Charles, who got spanked for being "(awfully) fresh" (**30** 20–21). Tellingly enough, Laurie comes home late when Charles had to stay after school, offering the poor excuse that "all the children stayed to watch him" (**31** 16–24). Similarly, when Charles is kept in for a second time, he again enjoys the company of his fellow-pupils, including Laurie (**32** 14–15), of course.

2. The narrator's perspective

When did Laurie's mother realize?

From the start Laurie's mother believes in Charles' separate existence, probably thinking that his misbehaviour is the result of somebody else's faulty child-rearing practices. This would explain why she and her husband are so interested in contacting "Charles' mother" at one of the PTA meetings (**31** 35–36, **32** 36–40, **33** 18–21) Laurie's tactics have undoubtedly proved to be extremely effective. When she finally approaches Laurie's teacher at the second PTA meeting, since "no one mentioned Charles", she still suspects nothing. It is only the final words in this little 'comedy' that contain the solution for her (the key moment or key event) and that probably make her realize what roles she and her husband were really playing in it.

3. The reader's perspective

When did you realize Laurie was not telling the whole truth?

[Answers will vary. The earliest hint is Laurie's hesitation when asked the boy's name (**30** 21); most readers will at least understand the significance of the teacher's remarks (**32** 32, 35–36).]

4. Dramatic irony

How did your knowledge affect your enjoyment of the story?

Knowing (or suspecting) the truth makes the whole situation seem ironic. You know (or suspect) what certain remarks mean, and can laugh at the mother's naive acceptance of everything her son tells her. Most readers will be amused at Laurie's large repertoire of psychological tricks. He seems to know exactly how and when to disquieten, to placate, to manipulate and to provoke his parents. In contrast to her son, Laurie's mother appears pretty helpless. Instead of using her intelligence and contacting Laurie's teacher to clear matters up as quickly as possible, she allows herself to be manoeuvred into a position which makes her strangely dependent on what her son deigns to offer her as far as life in the kindergarten is concerned. The ironic climax of the story is her confrontation with the teacher (**33** 26–**34** 3).

5. Surface humour

What else is funny about the story?

There is considerable humour in the accounts of Laurie/Charles' misbehaviour at school and his insolence at home — but also in the parents' strained efforts to seem calm and unconcerned (e.g. **30** 17, **32** 4, **33** 9).

Unit III
The Characters

1. Reader's sympathies

Which character do you sympathize with (laugh at) most? Why?

[Note that both verbs are slightly ambiguous:
sympathize with = identify with/feel sorry for;
laugh at = see as witty, clever, amusing/see as ridiculous.
This ambiguity can be exploited by the teacher.]

As likely as not, the students will prefer Laurie to any other character in this story. Seen from a juvenile's perspective, Laurie lives at an enviably free stage of life. The way he chooses to solve his conflicts is not viable for older children who, like adults, are more or less hedged in by numerous social conventions. Laurie's world is still ruled by unhampered feelings, the imaginative, and the spontaneous. Laurie at the age of 15 would probably have had to solve his conflicts in a more rational way. Even those readers who disapprove of Laurie/Charles' behaviour will not fail to be amused by this account of his exploits.

Alternative: Most of the humour is at the expense of the mother. But since we have direct access to her (the narrator's) thoughts and feelings, worries and fears, we cannot help sympathizing with her — even after we realize that she herself is the person she is so curious to meet: "Charles' mother".

2. The child's behaviour

Try to explain why Laurie/Charles behaved as he did.

Obviously, Laurie is unable at first to coordinate the potential of his awakening individuality with the restrictive rules of school life, most of which exist to make living in a group possible. He still has to learn how to assert himself in an effective manner, i.e. one which will not alienate others or lead to further repression. Instead, he vents his frustration on teacher and fellow-pupils alike — and even on his uncomprehending parents. The reasons for his failure to "adjust" (**33** 35) can only be guessed at. On the one hand, Laurie's sudden break with his nursery-school role (marked by a change of clothes and manners: **30** 1–6) is the result of a natural development. On the other hand, he may have been encouraged by his parents to expect too much of school life. Their 'permissive' style of child-rearing (cf. following question) may have been inadequate preparation for some unaccustomed forms of school discipline. It is also possible that the teacher may have been unnecessarily authoritarian (cf. **31** 2–4).

3. Parental attitudes
What do you think of the way the parents deal with Laurie?
On the face of it, there is nothing wrong with Laurie's parents. Both are tolerant, self-controlled and interested people. Tactfully, Laurie's mother tries to turn a blind eye to her son's provocations and impertinence to his father (**30** 13, **31** 1), presumably in the hope that he will calm down if ignored. Nor does his father let himself be provoked by Laurie's original but highly disrespectful form of address (**31** 26–27). Both parents are really concerned about what goes on in Laurie's class, in particular about Charles' "unsettling" influence. Still, their shortcomings cannot be overlooked. They are just about sensitive enough to see some connection between Laurie's aggressive attempts at self-assertion and his wild stories about Charles (**31** 11–13). However, they fail to put two and two together, even when Laurie comes home with the unlikely story that all the children stayed after school with Charles (**31** 24, **32** 15). They seem incapable of imagining that their own child may be the disturbing influence in question. Or they see life at home and life at school as two neatly separated spheres. Indeed, they never ask Laurie any questions about his own position in the kindergarten or his attitude towards this Charles.

4. Techniques of characterization [Optional at this point. This aspect can be reserved for treatment in connection with a later story, e.g. "Christmas Gift".]
In what way do you get to know what the characters are like?
[It would be best to deal with each character individually, picking out where we see them in action, and where the narrator interprets something for us.]
Summary: It is mainly through the dialogue that the persons in the story begin to take shape (dramatic presentation).
Apart from this, the story contains a few narrative passages (e.g. **30** 2–4; **31** 27, 35–6) which give the reader considerable insight into the narrator's state of mind during the conflict. An important element is her characterization through adjectives and adverbs of the way people speak and move: **30** 5, 8, 10, 16, 27; **31** 14, 39; **32** 12, 31; **33** 9, 30, 35. This 'interpretation' is however, based on what she sees — facial expressions, etc. — and is therefore consistent with the basically dramatic form of presentation.

Homework / Group work suggestions (Vocabulary):

1. Note down all words and phrases in the story which belong to the wordfield 'school/kindergarten'. Suggested items:
   a) types of school; b) teacher (activities); c) pupil (activities);
   d) school life.

[Note: One may take the opportunity and let the students find out more about the American school system. This could be expanded to a full 'Landeskunde' Unit.]

2. Note down all words and phrases referring to the characterization of persons. Suggested items:
a) behaviour; b) feelings.

James Thurber

The Princess and the Tin Box

Once upon a time, in a far country, there lived a king whose daughter was the prettiest princess in the world. Her eyes were like the cornflower, her hair was sweeter than the hyacinth, and her throat made the swan look dusty.

From the time she was a year old, the princess had been showered with presents. Her nursery looked like Cartier's window. Her toys were all made of gold or platinum or diamonds or emeralds. She was not permitted to have wooden blocks or china dolls or rubber dogs or linen books, because such materials were considered cheap for the daughter of a king.

When she was seven, she was allowed to attend the wedding of her brother and throw real pearls at the bride instead of rice. Only the nightingale, with his lyre of gold, was permitted to sing for the princess. The common blackbird, with his boxwood flute, was kept out of the palace grounds. She walked in silver-and-samite slippers to a sapphire-and-topaz bathroom and slept in an ivory bed inlaid with rubies.

On the day the princess was eighteen, the king sent a royal ambassador to the courts of five neighboring kingdoms to announce that he would give his daughter's hand in marriage to the prince who brought her the gift she liked the most.

The first prince to arrive at the palace rode a swift white stallion and laid at the feet of the princess an enormous apple made of solid gold which he had taken from a dragon who had guarded it for a thousand years. It was placed on a long ebony table set up to hold the gifts of the princess's suitors. The second prince, who came on a grey charger, brought her a nightingale made of a thousand diamonds, and it was placed beside the golden apple. The third prince, riding on a black horse, carried a great jewel box made of platinum and sapphires, and it was placed next to the diamond nightingale. The fourth prince, astride a fiery yellow horse, gave the princess a gigantic heart made of rubies and pierced by an emerald arrow. It was placed next to the platinum-and-sapphire jewel box.

Now the fifth prince was the strongest and handsomest of all the five suitors, but he was the son of a poor king whose realm had been overrun by mice and locusts and wizards and mining engineers so that there was nothing much of value left in it. He came plodding up to the palace of the princess on a plow horse and he brought her a small tin box filled with mica and feldspar and hornblende which he had picked up on the way.

The other princes roared with disdainful laughter when they saw the tawdry gift the fifth prince had brought to the princess. But she examined it with great interest and squealed with delight, for all her life she had been glutted with precious stones and priceless metals, but she had never seen tin before or mica or feldspar or hornblende. The tin box was placed next to the ruby heart pierced with an emerald arrow.

"Now," the king said to his daughter, "you must select the gift you like best and marry the prince that brought it."

The princess smiled and walked up to the table and picked up the present she liked the most. It was the platinum-and-sapphire jewel box, the gift of the third prince.

"The way I figure it," she said, "is this. It is a very large and expensive box, and when I am married, I will meet many admirers who will give me precious gems with which to fill it to the top. Therefore, it is the most valuable of all the gifts my suitors have brought me and I like it the best."

The princess married the third prince that very day in the midst of great merriment and high revelry. More than a hundred thousand pearls were thrown at her and she loved it.

Moral: *All those who thought the princess was going to select the tin box filled with worthless stones instead of one of the other gifts will kindly stay after class and write one hundred times on the blackboard 'I would rather have a hunk of aluminum silicate than a diamond necklace.'*

Biographical Notes

James Thurber is considered by many to be America's greatest 20th-century humorist. He was born in Columbus, Ohio in 1894. From early childhood, he suffered from bad eyesight. He was therefore prevented from joining the army in the First World War and worked as a government clerk instead.

After graduating from Ohio State University he held a number of jobs in the U.S.A. and abroad: he was on the staff of the American Embassy in Paris for two years and then worked as a journalist for several American daily newspapers. In 1926 he joined the staff of The New Yorker *– a famous American critical and satirical magazine. It was this magazine that first published most of his stories and cartoons.*

Altogether James Thurber published twenty books, most of them a mixture of cartoons, sketches, stories and essays. One of his favourite forms was the fable – it enabled him to make subtle and satirical points about the ways of the (modern) world.

He was twice married and divorced. In his later life he lived alone in Connecticut suffering from increasing blindness. He died in New York in 1961.

Annotations

36 6 **nursery** child's playroom or bedroom – **Cartier's** expensive French jeweller's shop, with branches in large cities all over the world – 7 **platinum** ['plætɪnəm] greyish-white metal, even more expensive than gold – **emerald, sapphire, topaz, ruby** (green, blue, yellow and red) precious stones – 8 **china dolls** dolls made of china (Porzellan) – **linen books** books covered in linen (Leinen), i.e. cheaper than leather-bound ones – 11 **rice** In Britain and America, a bride and groom are showered with rice and/or confetti. – 12 **lyre** ['laɪə] very old musical instrument with strings – 13 **blackbird** ['– –] singing bird with a yellow beak – **boxwood** wood of a small tree (Buchsbaum) – 14 **samite** ['sæmɪt] silk brocade – 15 **ivory** ['aɪvərɪ] a hard white substance from the tusks of elephants – **inlaid with rubies** with rubies set into the surface as a decoration – 16 **ambassador** [–'– – –] high-ranking diplomat – 20 **swift** quick – **stallion** ['stæljən] male horse – 22 **dragon** ['drægən] (in stories) fire-breathing animal – 23 **ebony** ['ebəni] hard black wood – **suitor** (old use) man wishing to marry a woman – 24 **charger** (old use) horse used in battles – 28 **astride** riding on – **gigantic** [dʒaɪ'gæntɪk] – 29 **to pierce** to make a hole through s.th. – 31 **handsome** good-looking – 32 **realm** [relm] kingdom – 33 **locust** ['ləʊkəst] insect that flies in great swarms and destroys crops – **wizard** ['wɪzəd] (in stories) man who has magic powers – **mining engineer** an expert in getting minerals out of the earth (Bergbauingenieur)

37 1 **to plod** to move slowly and heavily – 2 **mica, feldspar, hornblende** worthless stones which are pretty and colourful – 4 **disdainful** showing one's low opinion of s.o./s.th. – 5 **tawdry** cheap, lacking good taste – 6 **to squeal** to make a high-pitched sound – 7 **to glut with** to give too much of – 15 **to figure** *coll.* to see, to understand – 16 **admirer** person who finds s.o./s.th. beautiful or interesting – 17 **gem** [dʒem] polished precious stone – 19 **in the midst of** in the middle of – 20 **merriment** joyful laughter – **revelry** ['– – –] dancing, singing and feasting – 25 **hunk** large, rough piece – **aluminum silicate** a component of many rocks – **necklace** ['nekləs] string of jewels worn around the neck

Interpretation and Teaching Notes

Summary and Analysis

Thurber's "The Princess and the Tin Box" could be loosely categorized as 'a funny fairy tale'. It is, in fact, an ironic treatment of an established literary form, or more precisely, of two established literary forms: the fairy tale and the fable. Elements of the fairy tale predominate: the traditional "Once upon a time ..." opening ('Es war einmal ...'), the romantic setting, the far-away kingdom, the beautiful princess and her many suitors. The basic story-line is reminiscent of a number of different traditional tales. What brings Thurber's tale closer to the fable is that the moral is made explicit, and is set off from the text (as in many of the fables of La Fontaine, for example), lest the reader miss the point. Were "The Princess and the Tin Box" a traditional, serious tale, the moral might be, for instance, 'a man may be rich in attire but poor in spirit', 'all that glitters is not gold', 'money isn't everything', or even as in more current and popular tones, "Can't Buy Me Love". The point is, however, that the point of the story is not the expected one.

The story tells of a princess who has been surrounded since childhood with fantastic riches, toys and furniture made of gold and jewels, beautiful clothes, etc. At the age of eighteen she has to choose between five suitors — all princes — according to the gifts they bring her. The first four — on swift white stallion, grey charger, black and fiery yellow horses, respectively — all bring magnificent jewelled gifts. The fifth is the handsomest, but poor, and arrives on a ploughhorse. His offering, a tin box of worthless stones, fascinates the princess, who has never seen anything like it before. Nevertheless, she chooses one of the magnificent gifts for the most mercenary and cynical reasons imaginable, and of course marries the prince who brought it.

"The Princess and the Tin Box" is both humorous and satirically effective because neither the central character nor the author do or say what the reader would expect. The form, content, and language — supported by what one already knows about stories which begin with the formula "Once upon a time ..." — might seem to be leading up to the traditional "they lived happily ever after" ending and an affirmation of traditional values. Yet Thurber sets signals to warn even the non-overly sensitive reader that this way, his way, has different twists, and therefore the reader should be prepared for surprises. The 'moral of the story' is therefore on two levels. One is implicit in the story, and can be approximated by Oscar Wilde's witticism: "When I was young, I thought that money was the most important thing in life; now that I am old I know that it is." The other level is its translation into a direct 'reproach' to the 'naive' reader: When you (the reader) were young (beginning this story), you might have believed that there exist princesses who prefer love to money. Now that you are older (have finished the story), you should understand that this is not true. But, if you still haven't learned your lesson (were surprised that the princess did not choose the fifth prince), you are as naive and comical as the poor prince, and will be treated like a school child (in life and literature). The fact that this also applies to sophisticated readers who had been expecting *some* cynical twist to the story, but didn't know just what, adds to the impact of this tongue-in-cheek 'reproach'.

Thurber was above all a distinguished craftsman, and while the structure and language of the tale are at first sight rather straightforward, a number of subtle details reveal his craftsmanship. The brief introduction, with its traditional "Once upon a time ..." opening formula and its archaically-phrased (e.g. "like *the* cornflower") and romantically-lush images, serves to relax the reader, a necessity for the surprises that follow. One does not expect that the "prettiest princess in the world" will turn out to be a coldly calculating woman of urban-matron proportions.

Thurber's sparing use of anachronistic references (**36** 7: "Cartier's window"; **36** 33: "mining engineers") are a hint that we can expect this story to have an appropriately cynical moral for our materialistic times. By contrast, they also serve to point out that Thurber is deliberately overdoing the romanticism (e.g. **36** 2–4, 11–14). One may or may not notice that the archaic style is similarly exaggerated with its old-fashioned multiple linkings (**36** 7, 8 "... or ... or ... or ..."; **36** 33: "... and ... and ... and ...") and alliteration (**36** 14, **37** 1–2). The procession of *five* princes on five different kinds of horses with five different gifts also goes beyond what is usual: in most fairy tales, a series of three is considered enough to build up the required tension.

These elements of parody will have been spotted immediately by the readers of *The New Yorker*, where it first appeared. Readers of this magazine do not expect simple-minded moralistic tales; they do expect witty, sophisticated, ironic and even cynical pieces, and this is what Thurber gives them. He allows them to congratulate themselves on their ability to spot the irony and ambiguity — without of course giving the game away entirely. It may take time and several readings before a non-native reader can share in the fun to the same extent. But at least (and at the very latest) they will hardly fail to be struck by the incongruous tone of the princess's first (and only) utterance: "The way I figure it is this ..." (**37** 15). Two buddies chatting over their beers might speak like this, but hardly a princess in a fairy tale. As it turns out, her mercenary morality matches the tone. The return to the mock-romantic fairy-tale mode at the end (**37** 19–21; cf. also **10** 19–20) is then doubly incongruous, and makes clear what it was half-hiding, half-revealing all the time.

To sum up, the joke may be on the reader (even on the smartest of readers) but as long as one can see how it is being done, there is considerable enjoyment in being led up the garden path by Thurber.

Unit I
The Story's Effects on the Reader

Introductory Remarks:

— If non-native students are to enjoy the story, they should be helped to get the point the first time round, rather than after several readings. This does not mean they should anticipate the outcome, which contains an element of surprise even for experienced native readers, but rather that they should be helped from the start to get on the right wave-length, as it were, to appreciate Thurber's tongue-in-cheek humour. Not to get the joke is to resent the joke-telling. Hence the step-by-step presentation of the introduction, suggested here (points 1 and 2). Advanced students may, of course, proceed directly to point 3 and listen to the full recording right away.

— Ideally, the genuine fairy tale in this collection, "The Captive Princess", should have been read before this one is dealt with. This is not essential, however, as a certain familiarity with the traditional genre can be assumed.

— As in the case of "The Captive Princess", we recommend an oral presentation of the story. The remarks on page 20 apply here as well.

1. First paragraph (**36** 1–4)

What impression do you get of the story from its first paragraph?

The traditional opening "Once upon a time" makes you expect a romantic fairy tale. The "far country", the "king" and the beautiful "princess" are also typical of the fairy tale. Similarly the romantic comparisons with flowers and swans.

[Readers familiar with Thurber will notice the slight note of exaggeration here, but it is not necessary to point this out at this stage.]

2. Second and third paragraph (**36** 5–15)
What important fact do you learn about the princess here?
Is there anything about this account which sounds a bit strange for a fairy-tale?
The princess who has grown up in unimaginable luxury is a familiar figure in fairy tales. So is the list of precious stones, gold, ivory, etc. with which her wealth and status are stressed. The reference to platinum (**36** 7) — unknown until modern times — does seem a bit out of place, however. And there is one obvious anachronism: "Her nursery looked like Cartier's window" is a definite New York City allusion, which clashes with the archaic setting that went before it. Another 'false note' is the idea of throwing "real pearls" at a wedding instead of rice or confetti — not very pleasant for the bride, one might imagine.

3. Oral presentation of whole story

4. Comprehension and discussion
Describe as simply as possible what takes place in the story. [See "Summary."]
What did you expect to happen at the end?
Why did you expect this?
In spite of the various warnings (see point 2) that this story is in some way different, we still have the classic fairy tale situation: a princess brought up in unimaginable luxury and faced with the choice of one of the rich princes with magnificent gifts, or the poor prince with the worthless, purely symbolic gifts. Of course we expect the princess to realize that 'money is not everything' and to recognize the sincerity of this last prince, especially since he is "the strongest and handsomest" (**36** 31). Her delight (**37** 6) at his unusual gift reinforces this impression, so most readers will think at this point that her choice is a foregone conclusion.
At what point in the story did you realize that this would not happen?
What told you that this would not happen?
Was the princess' choice a real surprise ending?
Answers will vary widely. Even the most sophisticated readers are unlikely to guess what the "moral" will be in advance, but for some, the 'warnings' planted here and there (see point 2) will be enough to make them expect the story to take a cynical turn. Just what turn is difficult to guess, however.

Homework:

a) Write one hundred times in your exercise book "I would rather have a hunk of aluminum silicate than a diamond necklace". [Recommended for those teachers with an established reputation as practical jokers or sadists.]

or

b) Read the story, and pick out everything in it which is (not) typical of a fairy tale. [Two groups; cf. Unit II, 2.]

or

c) Write an alternative ending for the story, either as a serious fairy tale/ fable or as a funny version. [For advanced students; cf. Unit II, 4.]

Unit II
Fable, Fairy Tale and Parody

1. Comparison with familiar tales

What traditional stories does "The Princess and the Tin Box" remind you of?

It is not based on any one story, but contains elements of a number of familiar tales. Some examples:

— In the German tale "König Drosselbart", the princess has refused a number of rich princes who do not come up to her standards. Her father then says she has to accept the next suitor to come, no matter what he is like. A begger comes next, so she has to marry him. After she is cured of her haughtiness, he reveals that he is really a prince.

— In Shakespeare's *The Merchant of Venice*, Portia's suitors have to choose between three caskets, only one of which contains her picture. Two princes choose the gold and the silver caskets, respectively, and are rejected. Only Bassanio chooses the unpretentious lead casket and can marry Portia. This is probably based on a traditional tale.

2. The fairy tale

Most of these stories are classic fairy tales/Märchen.

Sum up all the details that make the Thurber story seem to be one. [Discussion of Homework]

— classic opening and closing formulae (**36** 1, **37** 19–21; cf. "Captive Princess", **6** 1, **10** 19–20)

— classic characters and setting

— classic situation

— archaic language (see "Summary and Analysis")

— repetitive sequence of events (**36** 20–**37** 3)

3. The fable

Is a 'moral' typical of a fairy tale?

All fairy tales have some moral to them, but it is seldom made explicit, and is often very vague — e.g. 'good triumphs over evil', as in "The Captive Princess".

An explicit moral is a mark of the *fable.*

What traditional fables do you know?

If the students do not come up with any, at least one classic example should be given. Most classic fables have animals as characters, but this is not essential. Their 'morals' are generally less romantic, and more realistic than those of fairy tales. Here are summaries of a few well-known La Fontaine fables:

The Grasshopper and the Ant: A grasshopper spent the summer playing and singing. When winter comes, she knocks on the ant's door, asking for food to tide her over till the spring, when she will pay her back. The self-righteous ant refuses, saying "You sang all the summer: now you can dance!"

The Frog who Wanted to be as Big as a Bull: A frog sees a bull and decides he would like to be just as big. He takes a deep breath and blows himself up until he bursts. Moral: The world is full of foolish people who have ideas beyond their station.

The Crow and the Fox: A fox sees a crow perched on a tree with a piece of cheese held in his beak. He tells the bird how beautiful his plumage is, and that he must have a beautiful voice to go with it. The crow opens his beak to show off, and drops the cheese, which is grabbed by the fox. The fox mocks him for his stupidity in listening to flattery.

The Wolf and the Lamb: A wolf accuses a lamb of disturbing his drinking water. Since the lamb is downstream from the wolf, he points out that this cannot be the case. The wolf ignores this, and adds a number of equally ridiculous accusations about the past activities of the lamb and/or his relations. The lamb's eminently reasonable replies do not save him from being eaten by the wolf. Moral: Might is Right.

4. 'Straight' version and parodies

What would the moral have been if this were a serious fairy tale?

What would the princess have been like?

For some more conventional 'morals', see "Summary and Analysis". Such a 'moral' would call for a different kind of princess from the one that emerges at the end of Thurber's tale. She would have to disdain the riches offered to her, and choose the poor prince for his goodness and sincerity (though his being handsome helps!). As a reward for her moral integrity, the prince would probably turn out to be rich after all.

What do you think a princess would do today?

[This will amount to thinking of other ways the fairy tale or fable forms could be parodied. Advanced students could be encouraged to formulate alternative 'morals for our time' as well as alternative endings, preferably as homework.]

Some suggestions:

— The princess marries the poor prince, saying "Everybody knows this is the way to get even richer". (Moral: Even princesses read fairy tales.)

— She marries one of the rich princes, divorces him, demands alimony, runs off with the poor but handsome prince, and lives happily ever after. (Moral: What's yours is mine, and what's mine is my own.)

— She marries the poor prince, saying "Who says I can't have all those jewels and a handsome prince as well?" (Moral: Princess's Lib has arrived.)

— She marries the poor prince, but he turns out to be a drug addict/gambler/Moonie/wife-beater (Moral: Happy endings have gone out of fashion.)

— She marries the poor prince, starts a terrorist campaign against mice, locusts and mining engineers, and has the time of her life. (Moral: Patty Hearst, eat your heart out!)

— She marries the poor prince, invests some of her riches in his impoverished kingdom, turns it into an industrial zone or tourist attraction, and gets even richer than she was before. (Moral: Judicious capital investment can pay dividends.)

Lord Dunsany

The Speech

"Crime," said the old journalist one night at his club. "One reads a good deal about violence nowadays; but I never read of a crime that would make a story like the one that there was when I was young. That would have made a story. But it was all hushed up."

"No doubt for some good reason," a younger journalist said.

"Yes," said the old journalist. "It had to be. They were extremely careful not to disturb the peace of Europe in those days. That, you see, was what the crime was about. There was a young man, scarcely remembered now, brilliant though he was – the Honourable Peter Minch. His old father you would never have heard of. A totally obscure old peer, Lord Inchingthwaite. But people heard of Peter Minch in his time. He was an M.P. and the coming man of the Opposition, one of those coming men that you never hear any more of.

"At the time that I tell about, he was going to make a speech in the House. Things had been simmering for some time. What this young fellow was going to say just at that time wasn't going to help the peace of Europe at all. What he was going to say would have prodded Austria pretty hard; and, if Germany had supported her in what would have been quite justifiable resentment, Russia would not have liked it, and the fat would have been in the fire. But there was no stopping Minch. He was a bit of a firebrand. The government couldn't stop him, of course. And as for the Opposition, he was their fancy man, and they were probably thinking more of how it would embarrass the government than how it would annoy the Austrians."

And then (the old journalist went on) the extraordinary thing happened. A man walked into the central office of Minch's party, without giving his name, and said quite clearly that he had sure information that was not exactly a message, and must not be taken as a threat but only a warning, that that speech would never be made.

"What do you mean?" said the Chairman of the Party.

"I mean," said the man, "that there is an organization with which I have nothing to do, nothing whatever, who are determined to stop that speech, and who are powerful enough to do what they threaten. It is not I that threaten. I came to warn you."

"Do you mean," said the Chairman, "that they are going to use force?"

"They will use whatever is necessary," said the stranger. "We – that is, they – consider war to be the greater evil."

"War?" said the Chairman. "Who says we are making war?"

"Their information," said the stranger, "is that what Mr Minch is going to say just at this time will bring war nearer. They are well-informed, and they have told me they are convinced that causing the death of one man is preferable to the risk of disturbing the peace of Europe."

Well, as politely as possible, the Chairman told him to go to hell. And as the man left, he said, "That speech will not be delivered. Under no circumstances will it be, in the House."

The Opposition told Scotland Yard. And they took the matter up at once, and assured the Chairman of the Party that the entire police force of the metropolis would be available. Police protection on an enormous scale was given to Minch at once.

I think Scotland Yard must have known more than they ever told about the organization that was making that threat, because they said at once that the man that had called on the Chairman of the Party would have been a man named Hosken. And that's who he turned out to be. The Chairman asked them then if they would arrest him. But the chief inspector said: Better not – better leave him at large, and he might give them more information. And he did.

The Chairman of the Party was sitting in his office with a burden removed from his mind, for he felt that the police had everything well in hand, when in walked this extraordinary man again. They let him come in, because they wanted to hear what the fellow had to say. They addressed him by his name this time, and I think it gave the Chairman a little childish pleasure to imply by doing so that they knew all about him.

"Well, Mr Hosken," said the Chairman, "is there anything more that you wished to tell us?"

A faint smile from Hosken greeted the use of his name. And then he said, "Only to say that all those policemen will not enable Mr Minch to make that speech and start a debate in Parliament, while things are as they are just now abroad."

"If Mr Minch desires to speak in the House, as he has every right to do, he will certainly do so," said the Chairman.

"I have come to say," said Hosken, "that if he will put it off, so as to give things time to simmer down, the powerful organization with which a friend of mine is in touch will take no action."

"If you mean by 'things' the state of affairs in Europe, we are not concerned with them. No one in Europe can deny us free speech," said the Chairman.

"It would be an open defiance," said Hosken. "And would lead to war."

"You must understand," the Chairman said to Hosken, "that we cannot tolerate any more blackmail."

"Certainly, sir," said Hosken. "Only there will be no speech in Parliament by Mr Minch for at least a week. And, if you stop him peacefully, there will be no need for violence."

Then he smiled and walked out.

Well, that's how things were (went on the old journalist) – tension rather acute, and this fiery young man going to start a debate in the House that would put all the fat in the fire, and perhaps set it overflowing and scalding all Europe, and a powerful organization of blackmailers – for they were nothing less – determined that that debate should never take place, and that one man's murder was nothing compared to war. And against the blackmailing gang was practically the whole of the police force of the metropolis. I needn't go into the precautions taken by the police. They took them all. Minch was constantly under observation by at least two of them. I doubt if anyone was ever more watched in London.

They soon ran Hosken down, but did not arrest him. All they did was to keep him under observation. I fancy they thought that he would be more useful to them that way.

On a Wednesday morning everything was all ready. Minch was going to speak at seven that evening. His whole family were going to be there, his old father in the Peers' Gallery, and all the rest of his family in the Ladies' Gallery. The police had a cab for Minch which was entirely bulletproof, even to windows of plate glass that was over an inch thick.

Well, the precautions were more than would have been taken for moving bullion from the Bank of England. They asked Minch to be at the House by 3 o'clock.

As he and his police escort arrived, a messenger boy handed a note to the inspector in charge of the guard. He opened it and saw an anonymous note, saying: *Mr Minch will not make that speech today.* He smiled, because once inside the precincts of the Houses of Parliament murder was quite impossible.

Minch's family were to arrive at half past six. At 3 o'clock, a dull debate opened. And yet the tension was electric, for everyone present knew the threat of the gang. The dignity of Parliament was at stake, and most of the members, even on the side to which Minch was going to cause so much trouble, put that first. Slowly the tension heightened, as the hands of the clock moved round to four.

And in that heightened tension everyone seemed to know what everyone else was thinking. They knew when any speaker was intending to be funny, and all laughed quickly and nervously, even before the little joke came.

And then, at five minutes past four, a note for Mr Minch was handed by a policeman to the inspector, who passed it to the sergeant-at-arms, who went into the chamber and gave it to Minch. Minch opened it and turned white.

"My father is dead," he said to a member beside him. "He's been murdered."

"I am terribly sorry," said the other man. "What happened?"

Minch handed the note to him. His father had been shot dead in his house. The murderer has escaped.

"And your speech," said the other member. "I am afraid –"

"No," said Minch. "That can't stop me. Nobody could be sorrier than I am. But private grief is one thing, public duty another."

"But, look here," said the other member. "I mean – you're a peer."

"I'm a what?" said Minch.

"You're a peer now," said the other again.

"My God!" Minch answered.

Well, that was the end of that. The gang had done it. They attacked as any man of sense would always attack, at the weakest point, where nobody was expecting it. And nobody did think of poor old Lord Inchingthwaite. He was quite obscure. But the moment he died, Peter Minch became a peer, and could make no more speeches of any sort in the House of Commons.

And he couldn't even make his speech in the House of Lords, until he had taken his seat, and all that took time. He did make the speech at a meeting that week in what had been his constituency, but Austria took no notice of that.

"So war was averted," said the young journalist.

"Well, yes," said the old journalist. "Not that it made any difference in the end."

Biographical Notes

Edward John Moreton Drax Plunkett was born in London in 1878 into an aristocratic Anglo-Irish family. He was educated at Eton and Sandhurst military academy. When his father died in 1899 he became the 18th Baron Dunsany. In 1904 he married Lady Beatrice Villiers, daughter of the Earl of Jersey.

Lord Dunsany fought in the Boer War (1899–1902) and in the First World War. His literary career began between these two wars. Together with W. B. Yeats he worked for the revival of the Irish theatre and one of his first plays, The Glittering Gates, *was produced by the Abbey Theatre, Dublin, in 1909. Later his plays were also produced by the Moscow Art Theatre as well as in England and America. He became Professor of English Literature in Athens, where he remained until the Germans occupied Greece in 1941. Back in Dublin and London, Lord Dunsany became a very prolific writer, producing numerous poems and stories for publication in the daily newspapers. The list of his literary works is a long one – in all, he had well over fifty books published.*

He travelled a lot, but most of his time he spent at his home, Dunsany Castle in County Meath, Ireland, or on his English estate, Dunstall Priory, in Kent. He died in Dublin in 1957.

Annotations

40 4 **to hush s.th. up** to prevent s.th. from becoming known to the public – 9 **the Honourable** title of a son or daughter of a Lord – 10 **obscure** not well known – **peer** nobleman entitled to sit in the House of Lords – 11 **M.P.** Member of Parliament – 15 **in the House** in the House of Commons – **to simmer** *here:* to be in a state of tension – 17 **to prod** *here:* to provoke – 18 **justifiable** with good reason, understandable – 19 **resentment** feeling of anger or bitterness after one has been treated badly – **the fat would have been in the fire** things would have been made much worse – 20 **firebrand** person who stirs up political quarrels; agitator – 22 **fancy man** a man who is useful for making a good impression on the public – 23 **to embarrass** [–'––] to make s.o. feel uncomfortable, to put in an awkward position – 24 **extraordinary** very unusual – 27 **threat** [θret] statement that one will harm or do violence to s.o. – 29 **chairman** someone in charge of a meeting; *here:* leader

41 3 **evil** ['i:vəl] *(n.)* s.th. very bad; disaster, misfortune – 10 **to deliver a speech** to make a speech – **under no circumstances** never, not at all – 13 **entire** complete, the whole – 14 **metropolis** large city, London – **on an enormous scale** much more than was usual – 21 **at large** free, uncontrolled, at liberty – 23 **burden** heavy load – 27 **to imply** [ɪm'plaɪ] to express indirectly – 31 **faint** weak – 37 **to put s.th. off** to delay s.th.; to decide to do s.th. at a later date – 38 **to simmer down** *here:* to become less exciting – 39 **in touch** in contact

42 2 **to deny s.o. s.th.** to refuse to give – 4 **defiance** [–'– –] action showing lack of respect for s.o.'s authority – 6 **blackmail** *here:* attempt to influence a person's behaviour by threatening violence – 11 **tension** state of excitement; feeling that something terrible is going to happen – 13 **to scald** to burn (with hot liquid) – 18 **to go into** to explain all the details of – **precautions** steps taken to avoid a possible danger – 21 **to run s.o. down** *here:* to look for and find – 27 **cab** taxi – **bulletproof** able to stop bullets (kugelsicher) – 30 **bullion** [ʊ] bars of gold or silver – 35 **inside the precincts** ['pri:sɪŋkts] within the walls – 39 **at stake** at risk, in danger

43 1 **to put s.th. first** to give most importance to – **to heighten** ['haɪtn] to become greater; to rise – 7 **sergeant-at-arms** *here:* officer whose duty it is to keep order – 16 **grief** great sorrow – 22 **any man of sense** any clear-thinking man/person – 29 **constituency** [–'– – – –] district that sends representatives to Parliament (Wahlkreis) – 31 **to avert** [ə'vɜ:t] to prevent, to stop from happening

Interpretation and Teaching Notes

Summary and Analysis

The classic detective story is bound by two fundamental rules. First, the reader must receive clues at the same time they are presented to, or discovered by, the story detective, the police, etc. Secondly, these clues should enable the reader, through a process of logical, if inspired, reasoning, to solve the crime. In this sense "The Speech" is a variant of the classic detective story (cf. 'Introduction', *Great Detective Stories*, Klett). However, the question here is not so much "whodunnit?" — that is, who is the murderer and what is the motive — but rather how it will be done.

The fact that the reader is subtly led astray, allowed to assume that the supposed victim is the actual victim, is also typical of this sub-genre. Have we, as readers, been fairly treated? Or have we been tricked, however cleverly? Certainly, compared with Scotland Yard, not to mention poor old Lord Inchingthwaite, we cannot complain.

An old, unnamed journalist, chatting about crime with younger journalists at their club, relates a story that took place in his younger days. It would have made such a good (news?) story then, but at the time it had been hushed up. It was kept quiet because the very peace of Europe (some time prior to World War I) was at stake.

At that time, a young, up-and-coming Member of the Opposition in Parliament — Peter Minch — was preparing to give a speech in the House of Commons. His speech would not only annoy the party in power, but would also severely annoy the Austrians and, in turn, the Germans and the Russians. War would be the likely result. An unidentified but powerful organization seeks to prevent this war by stopping the young M.P. from speaking. Three warnings (the traditional number!) are issued by the group. Two come orally from an emissary, a Mr Hosken. The third comes to Minch in the form of a note delivered a few hours before he is to speak in the Commons.

After each warning, the Opposition and Minch become even more determined to go ahead with the speech. Scotland Yard take all precautions, and Minch's security seems assured. Nothing and no one, it would appear, can prevent the speech. But then, just under three hours before the speech, word comes that Minch's father Lord Inchingthwaite has been murdered. Because the peerage is a hereditary one, the son automatically becomes the new Lord Inchingthwaite. Therefore, he may not deliver his speech in the Commons, his entry to the House of Lords takes time, and his presenting the speech outside of Parliament lessens its effect. All threats have been made good, and war has been averted, at least temporarily.

"The Speech" is a frame story, that is, a story within a story. It is thus heir to such classical story-sets as the *Canterbury Tales* or the *Decameron*, and kin to many lesser ones. (A similar technique is the 'present-day' frame of such stories of childhood reminiscences as "The Great Leapfrog Contest" or "The Pepper Tree".) That "The Speech" will be a frame story is clear as early as the second and third lines, made definite at line 14 ("At the time that I tell about ..."), and 'entered' at line 29 ("What do you mean?" ...). That this is dialogue from the story itself, and not from the frame becomes apparent at the moment we read, "said the Chairman of the Party." It is, therefore, a most effective transition. Throughout the story, the narrator (i.e. the "old journalist" of the 'frame") makes comments, and at one point (**42** 11–20) carefully sums up the plot, lest the reader and the 'audience' of journalists have missed anything. The story is left by using a frame transition similar to the entry transition (**43** 31). The reference to the war that was not averted (presumably World War I) brings us back to the frame, and that story's 'present' time. As is true of almost all frame stories, the form allows the author to present several points of view, to comment on the story itself, and to achieve an atmosphere very similar to that of the oral story-telling tradition.

The somewhat contrived plot (one might for example, question the assumption that any speech could, in real life, have such earth-shaking consequences) does not detract from the light, intellectual entertainment which this story provides. Readers of mystery stories are often asked to accept somewhat unlikely situations as probable, more or less, so that the 'game' can be played. As regards the fairness of this particular game, most of us will have to admit that we were not attentive enough. On reading the story a second time, we notice clues that were not correctly interpreted the first time. After all, that "totally obscure old peer" was brought to our attention at the very beginning of the story! And hardest of all to our pride as armchair sleuths is the best clue of all (**41** 10–11): that strange syntactical structure which emphasizes the dependent adverbial phrase, "in the House"! That one comma is (now) a clear indication that the speech could be given elsewhere. In fact, each warning could have led us to the correct solution, now that we think about it.

We as readers are nonetheless in good company. If the best of the Yard were fooled, then we — comparative innocents — may not be such fools after all. And we really may not have wanted to look too closely. Minch is not such an appealing character, risking millions of lives for the sake of a political point or two. And one might suspect that Scotland Yard share a few of our sympathies for the gang. It's sad, of course, about old Lord Inchingthwaite, but in a way, he did serve his country. Oh, and by the way, did you catch that old journalist's name? Did he say "Hopkins"? Or was it . . . Hosken?

Unit I
The Narrative Situation

Introductory Remarks:

— Since this story turns on a point of British parliamentary law, it would be advisable to ensure that the students have at least heard of the fact that a peer may not sit in the House of Commons. If this information has to be provided, it should be done very unobtrusively, and some time in advance of reading the story. This could be done either in a general lesson on the British system of government (cf. text 58 in *Modern Life*, Klett), or with regard to a particular case — like that of the left-wing Labour M.P. Tony Benn (formerly Sir Anthony Wedgewood-Benn, Viscount Stansgate) who gave up his peerage for this reason.

— We recommend that the recording be used (Klettnummer 57737) or that the story be read to the class (in appropriately melodramatic tones!).

— Whether or not the story is heard first, or read, more advanced classes might enjoy the story most if allowed to go through it completely once, without pausing for discussion.

— Teachers with a flair for the dramatic will find "The Speech" an appropriate vehicle. Simply writing "We'll kill, if necessary" on the blackboard before the class enters, for example, might well engender some curiosity as well as pre-class discussion. In any case, it should be noted that the socio-political elements in the story (war, freedom of speech, violence as a means to peace, etc.) are secondary to its enjoyment as a mystery story.

1. Listen to (or read) the story up to line 24. [Can also be set as homework in advance.]

2. Establishing the situation
What is happening at the beginning of the story?

The journalistic approach, so-called, might be appropriate here, with the traditional 'Who, where, what, when, why and how' series being asked. For example:

— Who is speaking at the beginning of the story? Name? Age? Profession? Nationality? Trustworthiness as witness?
— Who is he speaking to? Names, etc.?
— Where are they speaking? Location? Does the story take place in the same place(s)? If not, where?
— What is being talked about? Does the topic change?
— When does the discussion take place? Did what is being talked about take place at the same time? If not, when? Over what period of time?

Notice that any 'why' and 'how' questions should initially be restricted to the 'club' situation, e.g. Why is the speaker talking about this subject?

3. The frame story — a story within a story

Who is the narrator in this story?

Lord Dunsany is telling a story about an older journalist who is telling a story about ... So to answer this question we must first clarify which 'story' we are talking about. In the outer 'frame', about some journalists chatting in a London club, we have a detached author-narrator. One of these characters — the "old journalist" (**40** 1, 6, 24) — then becomes the narrator of the inner story.

'story' about journalists in their club,

story about Peter Minch,
told by the old journalist.

told by Lord Dunsany

[The above diagram could be sketched on the blackboard to clarify the 'frame' concept, which one will need to refer to occasionally in the course of the story, e.g. in connection with the passages **42** 11–20 and **43** 27–33.]

4. Effect of the 'frame story' technique

How else could the author have started telling the story about Peter Minch and his speech?

[If no suggestions are forthcoming, the teacher could provide the following 're-written' versions of the beginning as a basis for comparison. Advanced students could be asked to write versions in the style of the other stories in this volume.]

a) The author could have told this story directly in third-person form, without bothering about the journalists in their club, e.g.

— It was a time of great tension in Europe, when politicians had to be very careful not to disturb the peace. But Peter Minch, M.P., son of old Lord Inchingthwaite, was a bit of a firebrand ...

b) Alternatively, the author could have used the old journalist as first-person narrator right from the start, e.g.

— One reads a good deal about violence nowadays, but I never read of a crime that would make a story like the one that there was when I was young. That would have made a story. But it was all hushed up, because they were so careful not to disturb the peace of Europe in those days. That, you see is what the crime was about. There was a young man ...

What differences are there between these approaches?
Does one seem more natural than the others?
Which way, do you think, makes the story that follows sound true?

All of these approaches work fairly well. The a) version is the most neutral. There is no attempt to explain *why* anyone is telling this story, or where he got his information from — but this is quite common (7 of the 12 stories in this collection!) and we would have no trouble in accepting it.

Version b) makes it clear that the narrator himself remembers all this happening, but not why he is talking about it, and who he is talking to.

In Dunsany's story, we have in addition a plausible situation for the telling of the story. One could point out similar situations in real life, with somebody introducing an interesting piece of gossip about a mutual friend and trying in a similar way to kindle the listener's interest and curiosity. It also allows for the inclusion of some audience reactions at the beginning and end of the tale (**40** 5–6, **43** 31–33).

5. If time permits, listen to the recording of the complete story.

Homework: Read (or re-read) the complete story.

Unit II
Mystery and Suspense

1. Comprehension questions

Who is Peter Minch? (**40** 8–13, 21–23; note that emphasis is given to the fact that he is the son of a peer.)

What type of a man is he? (**40** 14–21, **43** 15–16; somewhat rash and arrogant in his willingness to risk war, but undeniably courageous, and willing to place principles he believes in over personal grief).

Why doesn't the organization want him to speak? (**41** 5–8)

What reasons are given for the Opposition's refusals to accept the warnings? (**40** 21–23, **41** 35–36, **42** 1–6)

In general, did most Members feel that Minch should be allowed to speak? (**42** 39 – **43** 1)

The organization gives three warnings, each in the form of a prophecy. What are they? (**41** 10–11, **42** 7–9, 34)

What action do the police take? Why isn't Hosken arrested? (**41** 12–22; **42** 16–23, 27–32) [In most English-speaking countries the police have powers to arrest only after a crime has been committed: *habeas corpus* effectively prevents imprisonment without specific criminal charges having been filed.]

How did the organization carry out their threats?

Why did this stop the speech? (**43** 11–30)

Did this stop the threat of war? (**43** 28–33)

2. The development of tension

How does the author manage to keep you interested in the story?

[Students can be asked to pick out the specific lines/passages which keep the reader's attention by heightening the tension; these can be either put on the board in the order they appear or grouped by topics.]

— (**40** 1–4) Old journalist's reference to crime, violence and official secrecy catches reader's attention and excites curiosity.
— (**40** 6–8, 14–20) Reference to the special nature of the crime, its connection with the danger of war.
— (**40** 30 – **41** 11) Passage presenting the terrorist organization's determination to prevent the speech, by killing if necessary – first inkling of what the "crime" might be.
— (**41** 12–15) Reference to massive police precautions — stresses the reality of the danger.
— (**41** 31–34) Hosken's confidence adds to the tension.
— (**42** 11–20) Here the narrator tells us directly that the "tension was acute", and sums up the tense situation.
— (**42** 24–31) Approaching the time of the planned speech, details of the massive police precautions and the apprehension of everybody involved.
— (**42** 32–33) Reminder of the gang's determination and confidence.
— (**42** 38–39; **43** 1–5) More direct statements about the tension and examples of people's nervousness.
— and then the crime (**42** 6–26), in spite of all precautions.

The sequence and timing of these references has obviously been carefully thought out. Note that each explicit mention of the tense situation comes closer together. The traditional trio of warnings also serves to build up tension, as each warning remains so self-confident in tone. Also, the very weight of the questions involved — i.e. war, murder, freedom of speech, blackmail — heightens the tension as the narrator constantly reminds his audience what is at stake. Finally, there is the polite tone and behaviour of all involved — Hosken is not crude, does not scream threats, the Chairman of the Opposition "as politely as possible" (**41** 9) tells him to go to hell, the police do not beat information out of Hosken, polite forms are used – Mr Hosken, Mr Minch, "Certainly, sir," (**42** 7). This air of (British?) reserve and politeness adds to the tension by its contrast with the possibility of war and murder.

3. The mystery element

Did you guess how the story would end?

[As indicated in the Summary and Analysis, a second reading does make better sleuths of us all; once we know what happened it is clear what will happen. Teachers might wish, therefore, to admit that they were fooled themselves the first time round, as a means of furthering discussion.]

Now that we know what happened, what clues were given in the story that might have led us to the correct victim?

Early references to Minch's "obscure" father (**40** 10–11); the intentional ambiguity (marked by syntax) of "Under no circumstances will it be, in the House" (**41** 10–11) as well as other prophecics; the reminder (**42** 25–26) of Minch's aristocratic family; the more specific reference (**42** 37) to what time the family would arrive, which on first reading seems irrelevant to the plot. Also relevant is the information that a crime *was* committed (**40** 2–3) and that Peter Minch was at least not murdered (**40** 12–13); the historical knowledge that a war was not caused by a speech in Parliament by an M.P. named Peter Minch.

4. Free discussion

- *On page 42, the stranger (Hosken) says "We — that is, they — consider war to be the greater evil." Remember that it is the old journalist who tells us what Hosken said. Do you think that Hosken made the slip of the tongue, or the old journalist? Why?*
- *How do you interpret/react to the last sentence in the story, "Not that it made any difference in the end"?*
- *On page 41, mention is made of the group's belief that "the death of one man is preferable to the risk of disturbing the peace of Europe." Do you agree or disagree with this belief? And what if you were that one person?*

Robert Turner

Christmas Gift

There was no snow and the temperature was a mild sixty-eight degrees and in some of the yards nearby the shrubbery was green, along with the palm trees, but still you knew it was Christmas Eve. Doors on the houses along the street held wreaths, some of them lighted. A lot of windows were lighted with red, green and blue lights. Through some of them you could see the lighted glitter of Christmas trees. Then, of course there was the music, which you could hear coming from some of the houses, the old familiar songs, *White Christmas, Ave Maria, Silent Night.*

All of that should have been fine, because Christmas in a Florida city is like Christmas any place else, a good time, a tender time. Even if you're a cop. Even if you pulled duty Christmas Eve and can't be home with your own wife and kid. But not necessarily if you're a cop on duty with four others and you're going to have to grab an escaped con and send him back, or more probably have to kill him because he was a lifer and just won't *go* back.

In the car with me was McKee, a Third-Grade, only away from a beat a few months. Young, clear-eyed, rosy-cheeked. All-American boy type and very, very serious about his work. Which was fine; which was the way you should be. We were parked about four houses down from the rented house where Mrs Bogen and her three children were living.

At the same distance the other side of the house was a sedan in which sat Lieutenant Mortell and Detective First-Grade Thrasher. Mortell was a bitter-mouthed, needlethin man, middle-aged and with very little human expression left in his eyes. He was in charge. Thrasher was a plumpish, ordinary guy, an ordinary cop.

On the street in back of the Bogen house, was another precinct car, with two other Firsts in it, a couple of guys named Dodey and Fischman. They were back there in case Earl Bogen got away from us and took off through some yards to that other block. I didn't much think he'd get to do that.

After a while McKee said: "I wonder if it's snowing up north. I'll bet the hell it is." He shifted his position. "It don't really seem like Christmas, no snow. Christmas with palm trees, what a deal!"

"That's the way it was with the first one," I reminded him.

He thought about that. Then he said: "Yeah. Yeah. That's right. But I still don't like it."

I started to ask him why he stayed down here, then I remembered about his mother. She needed the climate; it was all that kept her alive.

"Y'know," McKee said then. "Sarge, I been thinking; this guy Bogen must be nuts."

"You mean because he's human? Because he wants to see his wife and kids on Christmas?"

"Well, he must know there's a *chance* he'll be caught. If he is, it'll be worse for his wife and kids, won't it? Why the hell couldn't he just have *sent* them presents or something and then called them on the phone? Huh?"

"You're not married, are you, McKee?"

"No."

"And you don't have kids of your own. So I can't answer that question for you."

"I still think he's nuts."

I didn't answer. I was thinking how I could hound the stinking stoolie who had tipped us about Earl Bogen's visit home for Christmas, all next year, without getting into trouble. There was a real rat in my book, a guy who would stool on something like that. I was going to give him a bad time if it broke me.

Then I thought about what Lieutenant Mortell had told me an hour ago. "Tim," he said. "I'm afraid you're not a very good cop. You're too sentimental. You ought to know by now a cop can't be sentimental. Was Bogen sentimental when he crippled for life that manager of the finance company he stuck up on his last hit? Did he worry about *that* guy's wife and kids? Stop being a damned fool, will you, Tim?"

That was the answer I got to my suggestion that we let Earl Bogen get in and see his family and have his Christmas and catch him on the way out. What was there to lose, I'd said. Give the guy a break, I'd said. I'd known, of course, that Mortell wouldn't have any part of that, but I'd had to try anyhow. Even though I knew the lieutenant would think of the same thing I had – that when it came time to go, Bogen might be twice as hard to take.

McKee's bored young voice cut into my thoughts: "You think he'll really be armed? Bogen, I mean."

"I think so."

"I'm glad Mortell told us not to take any chances with him, that if he even makes a move that looks like he's going for a piece, we give it to him. He's a smart old cop, Mortell."

"That's what they say. But did you ever look at his eyes?"

"What's the matter with his eyes?" McKee said.

"Skip it," I said. "A bus has stopped."

We knew Earl Bogen had no car; we doubted he'd rent one or take a cab. He was supposed to be short of dough. A city bus from town stopped up at the corner. When he came he'd be on that, most likely. But he wasn't on this one. A lone woman got off and turned up the Avenue. I let out a slight sigh and looked at the radium dial of my watch. Ten-fifty. Another hour and ten minutes and we'd be relieved; it wouldn't happen on our tour. I hoped that was the way it would be. It was possible. The stoolie could have been wrong about the whole thing. Or something could have happened to change Bogen's plans, or at least to postpone his visit to the next day. I settled back to wait for the next bus.

McKee said: "Have you ever killed a guy, Sarge?"

"No," I said. "I never had to. But I've been there when someone else did."

"Yeah? What's it like?" McKee's voice took on an edge of excitement. "I mean for the guy who did the shooting? How'd he feel about it?"

"I don't know. I didn't ask him. But I'll tell you how he looked. He looked as though he was going to be sick to his stomach, as though he should've been but couldn't be."

"Oh," McKee said. He sounded disappointed.

"How about the guy that was shot? What'd he do? I've never seen a guy shot."

"Him?" I said. "Oh, he screamed."

"Screamed?"

"Yeah. Did you ever hear a child scream when it's had a door slammed on its fingers? That's how he screamed. He got shot in the groin."

"Oh, I see," McKee said, but he didn't sound as though he really did. I thought that McKee was going to be what they called a good cop – a nice, sane, completely insensitive type guy. For the millionth time I told myself that I ought to get out. Not after tonight's tour, not next month, next week, tomorrow, but right now. It would be the best Christmas present in the world I could give myself and my family. And at the same time I knew I never would do that. I didn't know exactly why. Fear of not being able to make a living outside; fear of winding up a burden to everybody in my old age the way my father was – those were some reasons but not the whole thing. If I talk about how after being a cop so long it gets in your blood no matter how you hate it, that sounds phony. And it would sound even worse if I said one reason I stuck was in hopes that I could make up for some of the others, that I could do some good sometimes.

"If I get to shoot Bogen," McKee said, "he won't scream."

"Why not?"

"You know how I shoot. At close range like that, I'll put one right through his eye."

"Sure, you will," I told him. "Except that you won't have the chance. We'll get him, quietly. We don't want any shooting in a neighborhood like this on Christmas Eve."

Then we saw the lights of the next bus stop up at the corner. A man and a woman got off. The woman turned up the Avenue. The man, medium height but very thin, and his arms loaded with packages, started up the street.

"Here he comes," I said. "Get out of the car, McKee."

We both got out, one on each side. The man walking toward us from the corner couldn't see us. The street was heavily shaded by strings of Australian pine planted along the walk.

"McKee," I said. "You know what the orders are. When we get up to him, Thrasher will reach him first and shove his gun into Bogen's back. Then you grab his hands and get the cuffs on him fast. I'll be back a few steps covering you. Mortell'll be behind Thrasher, covering him. You got it?"

"Right," McKee said.

We kept walking, first hurrying a little, then slowing down some, so that we'd come up to Bogen, who was walking toward us, just right, before he reached the house where his family was but not before he'd passed Mortell and Thrasher's car.

When we were only a few yards from Bogen, he passed through an open space, where the thin slice of moon filtered down through tree branches. Bogen wore no hat, just a sport jacket and shirt and slacks. He was carrying about six packages, none of them very large but all of them wrapped with gaudily colored paper, foil and ribbon. Bogen's hair was crew-cut, instead of long the way it was in police pictures and he'd grown a mustache; but none of that was much of a disguise.

Just then he saw us and hesitated in his stride. Then he stopped. Thrasher, right behind him, almost bumped into him. I heard Thrasher's bull-froggy voice say: "Drop those packages and put your hands up, Bogen. Right now!"

He dropped the packages. They tumbled about his feet on the sidewalk and two of them split open. A toy racing car was in one of them. It must have been still slightly wound up because when it broke out of the package, the little motor whirred and the tiny toy car spurted across the sidewalk two or three feet. From the other package, a small doll fell and lay on its back on the sidewalk, its big, painted eyes staring upward. It was what they call a picture doll, I think; anyhow, it was dressed like a bride. From one of the other packages a liquid began to trickle out onto the sidewalk and I figured that had been a bottle of Christmas wine for Bogen and his wife.

But when Bogen dropped the packages, he didn't raise his hands. He spun around and the sound of his elbow hitting Thrasher's face was a sickening one. Then I heard Thrasher's gun go off as he squeezed the trigger in a reflex action, but the flash from his gun was pointed at the sky.

I raised my own gun just as Bogen reached inside his jacket but I never got to use it. McKee used his. Bogen's head went back as though somebody had jolted him under the chin with the heel of a hand. He staggered backward, twisted and fell.

I went up to Bogen with my flash. The bullet from McKee's gun had entered Bogen's right eye and there was nothing there now but a horrible hole. I moved the flash beam just for a moment, I couldn't resist it, to McKee's face. The kid looked very white but his eyes were bright with excitement and he didn't look sick at all. He kept licking his lips, nervously. He kept saying: "He's dead. You don't have to be worrying about him, now. He's dead."

Front door lights began to go on then in nearby houses and people began coming out of them. Mortell shouted to them: "Go on back inside. There's nothing to see. Police business. Go on back inside."

Of course, most of them didn't do that. They came and looked, although we didn't let them get near the body. Thrasher radioed back to Headquarters. Mortell told me: "Tim, go tell his wife. And tell her she'll have to come down and make final identification for us."

"Me?" I said. "Why don't you send McKee? He's not the sensitive type. Or why don't you go? This whole cute little bit was your idea, anyhow, Lieutenant, remember?"

"Are you disobeying an order?"

Then I thought of something. "No," I told him. "It's all right. I'll go."

I left them and went to the house where Bogen's wife and kids lived. When she opened the door, I could see past her into the cheaply, plainly-furnished living room that somehow didn't look that way now, in the glow from the decorated tree. I could see the presents placed neatly around the tree. And peering around a corner of a bedroom, I saw the eyes, big with awe, of a little girl about six and a boy about two years older.

Mrs Bogen saw me standing there and looked a little frightened. "Yes?" she said. "What is it?"

I thought about the newspapers, then. I thought: "What's the use? It'll be in the newspapers tomorrow, anyhow." Then I remembered that it would be Christmas day; there wouldn't *be* any newspapers published tomorrow, and few people would bother about turning on radios or television sets.

"Don't be alarmed," I told her, then. "I'm just letting the people in the neighborhood know what happened. We surprised a burglar at work, ma'am, and he ran down this street. We caught up with him here and had to shoot him. But it's all over now. We don't want anyone coming out, creating any more disturbance, so just go back to bed, will you please?"

Her mouth and eyes opened very wide. "Who – who was it?" she said in a small, hollow voice.

"Nobody important," I said. "Some young hood."

"Oh," she said then and I could see the relief come over her face and I knew then that my hunch had been right and Bogen hadn't let her know he was coming; he'd wanted to surprise her. Otherwise she would have put two and two together.

I told her goodnight and turned away and heard her shut the door softly behind me.

When I went back to Mortell I said: "Poor Bogen. He walked into the trap for nothing. His folks aren't even home. I asked one of the neighbors and she said they'd gone to Mrs Bogen's mother's and wouldn't be back until the day after Christmas."

"Well, I'll be damned," Mortell said, watching the men from the morgue wagon loading Bogen onto a basket.

"Yes," I said. I wondered what Mortell would do to me when he learned what I'd done and he undoubtedly would, eventually. Right then I didn't much care. The big thing was that Mrs Bogen and those kids were going to have their Christmas as scheduled. Even when I came back and told her what had happened, the day after tomorrow, it wouldn't take away the other.

Maybe it wasn't very much that I'd given them but it was something and I felt a little better. Not much, but a little.

Biographical Notes

Robert Turner was born in New York City in 1915. He left school at 14 and joined the messenger service at New York University. He soon became a supervisor, and stayed at this job for ten years in all. He began writing crime stories for popular magazines and then worked as an editor for such a magazine. He became quite successful in this field: among other things, he founded a literary agency in New York, and was elected regional vice-president of the professional organization Mystery Writers of America.

Over the years he published a number of books (fiction and non-fiction) under various pseudonyms – for example, he wrote a series of three books on the activities of the Mafia under the pseudonym 'Don Romano'. He also wrote the scripts for several very popular television series (e.g. "Johnny Midnight", "Tombstone Territory"). Some of his stories have also been adapted for television. He now lives in Hollywood.

Annotations

46 1 **sixty-eight degrees** 68° Fahrenheit = 20° C – 2 **shrubbery** [ʌ] low bushes – 4 **wreath** circular arrangement of leaves; *here:* an American Christmas decoration – 10 **tender** friendly, loving, sympathetic – 11 **cop** *Am. sl.* policeman – **to pull duty** *sl.* to be on duty; to have to work – 13 **to grab** to catch – **con** *sl.* convict, prisoner – 14 **lifer** *sl.* person who has been sent to prison for life – 16 **Third-Grade** *Am.* policeman's rank – **beat** area guarded by policeman on foot (work done only by the lowest grade of policemen) – 21 **sedan** [sə'dæn] *Am.* car for four or more passengers – 22 **lieutenant** [lu:'tenənt] *Am.* high-ranking police officer – 24 **in charge** responsible (for s.th.) – **plumpish** [ʌ] rather plump (fat) –26 **precinct car** ['pri:sɪŋkt] *Am.* patrol car used to control a certain district of a town – 31 **to shift** to change (position) – 32 **What a deal!** What bad luck! How awful!

47 5 **Sarge** [sɑ:dʒ] *sl.* sergeant – 6 **to be nuts** *sl.* to be mad, crazy – 17 **to hound** to persecute, to be mean to – **stoolie** *Am. sl.* police informer (Spitzel); (also verb: 'to stool') – 19 **in my book** *coll.* as far as I am concerned; to me – 20 **if it broke me** even if it ruined me – 26 **to stick up** *sl.* to rob by threatening with a gun – **hit** *sl.* crime – 30 **a break** *coll.* a fair chance – 31 **wouldn't have any part of** would not have anything to do with – 38 **to go for a piece** *sl.* to reach for a gun

48 2 **skip it** *coll.* forget about it – 3 **doubted** did not think – **cab** *Am.* taxi – 4 **dough** [dəʊ] *Am. sl.* money – 7 **sigh** [saɪ] sound expressing disappointment, sadness or relief – 8 **to be relieved** *here:* to be let off duty by the arrival of the next patrol – 11 **to postpone** to put off – 16 **edge** *here:* sharp sound – 27 **groin** Leistengegend – 30 **sane** mentally healthy – **insensitive** [–'– – –] not having any feelings – 35 **to wind up** to end up – **burden** heavy load – 38 **phony** *coll.* not true; insincere – 39 **to stick** *coll.* to endure, to tolerate, to hold out – **to make up for** to compensate for

49 3 **at close range** from a short distance – 14 **string** *here:* line – 15 **pine** evergreen tree – 17 **to shove** [ʌ] *coll.* to push – 18 **cuffs** *here:* handcuffs, i.e. joined metal rings for fastening a person's hands – 19 **to cover** *here:* to stand with a gun in order to protect s.o. – 28 **slacks** loose-fitting trousers – 30 **gaudy** bright and showy – **foil** thin, metallic paper – **crew-cut** cut very close to the scalp – 32 **disguise** [dɪs'gaɪz] costume or mask hiding one's real appearance – 33 **stride** long step – 35 **bull-froggy** loud and unpleasant – 40 **to whirr** [wɜ:] to move with a buzzing sound

50 3 **a bride** woman getting married – 4 **liquid** ['lɪkwɪd] substance which can flow like water – **to trickle** to flow in drops or in a thin stream – **to figure** ['fɪgə] to guess, to come to the conclusion – 7 **to spin around** to turn round fast – 8 **to squeeze the trigger** to fire a gun – 12 **to jolt** [əʊ] to knock sharply – **heel** *here:* back part – **to stagger** to move unsteadily – 13 **to twist** to turn – 14 **flash** *here:* flashlight, torch – 16 **to resist** *here:* to stop oneself – 29 **cute** *Am. coll.* pleasant, attractive – 35 **glow** soft light – 36 **neat** tidy – 37 **to peer** to look very carefully – 38 **awe** [ɔ:] feeling of respect mixed with fear

51 4 **to bother about** to be interested in, to take the trouble to do s.th. – 6 **burglar** thief who breaks into houses – 7 **ma'am** [mæm] short for 'Madam' (respectful form of address) – 11 **hollow** *here:* with a quality of emptiness – 12 **hood** [hʊd] *Am. sl.* criminal – 14 **hunch** *coll.* suspicion, intuitive idea – 15 **to put two and two together** *coll.* to draw an obvious conclusion – 23 **morgue wagon** [mɔ:g] *Am.* car in which dead bodies are transported – 26 **eventually** at last, in the end – 28 **scheduled** ['ʃedju:ld] planned

Interpretation and Teaching Notes

Summary and Analysis

From the critical perspective of the 1980s, "Christmas Gift" is a set piece from the 'hard-boiled cop with a hidden heart of gold' school of detective story writing. Its mixture of brutal 'realism' and street-wise, idiomatic dialogue is patterned on the Dashiell Hammett formula (cf. *Great Detective Stories*, Klett) made internationally popular by Raymond Chandler. Were "Christmas Gift" a 1950s film brought back for television re-runs, a blurb in the TV-programme listings such as "Cop Bogart plays Santa to police-slain con's family", would tell the many aficionados of this genre what to expect. Much of our enjoyment in reading this story today, in fact, can be traced to our familiarity with its character types and conventions.

The story unfolds on Christmas Eve in "a Florida city" with a contrast between what should be — e.g. snow and "a tender time" (**46** 10) — and what is: a summer-like climate, and a police stake-out. The 'story so far' is quickly and dramatically filled in by the narrator, a police sergeant named Tim. It should be like Christmas:

> But not necessarily if you're a cop on duty with four others and you're going to have to grab an escaped con and send him back, or more probably have to kill him because he was a lifer and just won't *go* back. (**46** 12–15)

The policemen, all detectives, are introduced and described by the narrator in order of their importance to the story: McKee (young and trigger-happy), Mortell (the cynical lieutenant in charge who has 'seen it all'), Trasher ("a plumpish ordinary guy, an ordinary cop"), and "a couple of guys named Dodey and Fischman". There are, it should be noted, a total of six policemen. The police have received a tip that Bogen, the escaped convict, will visit his wife and three children on Christmas Eve. He is expected to be armed (**47** 34–39) and dangerous (**46** 14–15, **47** 23–25). The policemen are paired in cars (Tim and McKee, Mortell and Thrasher, Dodey and Fischman) with the last car parked on the street behind the house. Lt. Mortell's plan (**49** 16–20) is to surprise Bogen when he arrives from a bus stop, on foot. Thrasher will shove a gun into Bogen's back, McKee put the handcuffs on, while Tim and Mortell cover their partners. No chances are to be taken.

About an hour before midnight (**48** 7), Bogen steps off a city bus, his arms loaded with Christmas gifts, and the plan goes into action. But when

Thrasher tells Bogen to drop the packages and put his arms up, Bogen uses the opportunity to drop the packages and put his elbow into Thrasher's face. Thrasher's gun goes off accidentally (and ineffectually). Before Tim can use his own gun (**50** 10–11), and just as Bogen is reaching for his, McKee has shot Bogen in the right eye. Tim is ordered to tell Bogen's family what has happened. He lies to Mrs Bogen, saying that a young burglar, "nobody important" (**51** 12), had been shot. He also lies to Mortell, telling him that, after all, the Bogen family had not been at home. It would not be until the day after Christmas, when Tim returned, that the Bogen family would know what had really happened. "Maybe it wasn't much that I'd given them but it was something and I felt a little better" (**51** 31–32), Tim concludes.

The readers of this story sit with the policemen (as Tim's mental partners, so to speak), awaiting the not unexpected, distasteful outcome. How exactly it will happen provides the suspense. Most readers will have identified McKee, with much help from the author, as the stock characterization of the young, insensitive, and near-psychotic cop. How Tim will react when it happens fulfills the action sequence.

Ironic comparisons and contrasts are offered throughout the story, parallel to the 'peace on earth' versus 'cops and violence' theme. Tim doesn't like being a policeman, but will not quit (**48** 30–40), for instance. A "good cop" is a "nice, sane, completely insensitive type guy" (**48** 29–30). A violent criminal brings his children presents. Other contrasts of this type: McKee's face before and after the killing (**46** 17, **50** 16–18), and of course the eyes of the dropped doll and the eyes of Bogen's little daughter (**50** 2, 37–38). The effect of such ironies is probably dependent upon how familiar they are to students (who have certainly seen more shoot-outs in films and on TV than Mortell, or McKee, in their wildest dreams). The story is a well-done example of what is today a very popular genre, in both the written and visual media. Its structure and style have a taste of the dramatic script, and from today's perspective, it edges a bit towards melodrama, or even parody. What saves it from such a condemnation is our very familiarity with the type, and our nostalgic affection for it.

Unit I
Characterization

Preparation: Students should have read up to **49** 12.

1. The main characters

Name the main characters. Give short descriptions of each.

[Dodey and Fischman are almost 'extras', and Mrs Bogen and her children appear in minor roles at the end of the story. Therefore, in the order they appear, and also in order of importance, the main characters are Tim, Bogen, McKee, Mortell, and Thrasher.]

— *Tim* is an experienced police detective with the rank of sergeant. He dislikes much of his duties as a policeman (**48** 30–40), but stays on for want of a real alternative. He is married and has one child (**47** 12, **48** 33). His lieutenant, Mortell, says that he is "not a very good cop" (**47** 23–24) because he is too sentimental, and he himself seems to agree. We do not know his last name, or even what he looks like. Although his speech if filled with slang vocabulary, it is otherwise grammatical.

— *Bogen* (first name: Earl) is an escaped convict who had been serving a life-sentence for robbery and assault with intent to kill (**46** 14, **47** 25–26). He is probably armed (**47** 34–39), and not willing to be caught and returned to prison. He is of medium height but very thin with crew-cut hair and dressed in a sport jacket and shirt and slacks (**49** 9–10, 28, 30). He seems to have some affection for his family, bringing them Christmas gifts at the risk of being caught.

— *McKee* (no first name is given) is a very green detective, just having left the uniformed police (**46** 16–17). He is "young, clear-eyed, rosy-cheeked", an "All-American boy type" (a rather sarcastic reference to the clean-cut sporty ideal). He is probably not well-educated, and probably originally from the North (**46** 30). He seems fascinated by death and killing (**48** 13–28), and is "a completely insensitive type guy" (**48** 30). We would term him 'trigger-happy' at best; at worst, psychotic.

— *Mortell* (no first name) is "a bitter-mouthed, needlethin" middle-aged lieutenant, who has 'seen it all' or at least enough so that he has lost whatever emotions he once had (**46** 22–24, **47** 38–40). He might have once been like Tim.

— *Thrasher* (no first name) is an experienced detective (First-Grade), "a plumpish, ordinary guy, an ordinary cop" (**46** 24–25). He seems to be a bit clumsy, and has a "bull-froggy voice" (**49** 33–36, **50** 8–9).

2. Reader's sympathies

Which of these characters do you have sympathy for? Why?

The most likely choice is Tim. Mrs Bogen and her children — though barely referred to at this point in the story — may be mentioned as the only characters really deserving sympathy. Some may sympathize with Bogen himself — the 'under-dog' as it were, hunted, excluded from humanity. Though a violent man, a convicted criminal, he does show affection for his family.

No matter which character is chosen, it will be seen that all of the major characters are painted in grey tones, even the narrator. Tim is neither as cynical and hardened as Mortell, nor as fascinated by his potential power as McKee. But he is willing to step 'outside of the law' (**47** 17–21), to take advantage of his power as a policeman. He accepts that he is too sentimental to be "a good cop", as defined by Mortell. He recognizes his own dilemma, but continues to be a policeman. He says that he hopes to make a bad situation a bit better, but this might just be an excuse for not having the courage to leave his job.

3. Techniques of characterization

Examine the way we get to know what the characters are like. Take McKee (or Thrasher or Mortell) first as an example, and list what we are told explicitly about him, and how he is seen to behave.

[This question could also serve as board work, homework or group work. In each case a simple chart could be constructed to separate the explicit statements about this character from what is shown of his behaviour. Since both are filtered through the narrator's consciousness, one cannot always make a clear distinction, but it is useful to see how both techniques complement each other.]

Explicit statements about McKee: **46** 16–18, **47** 34, **48** 28–30, **50** 28

McKee in action: **46** 30 – **47** 16; **47** 34 – **48** 2; **48** 13–28; **50** 10–20

What about the narrator, Tim?

[In the case of the narrator, it is a lot more difficult to make such a distinction, since everything in the story is in some way relevant. But some passages are more revealing than others.]

Other character's statements about Tim: **47** 23–27

Tim's statements about himself: **48** 30–40

Particularly relevant thoughts and actions: **47** 7–15, 17–21, 28–29; **50** 32 – **51** 32

[Optional] *Imagine that you are making a film/television thriller based upon the characters in this story. Which actors would you choose [living or dead] to play the main roles?*

Some likely candidates: James Cagney, Humphrey Bogart, Gene Hackman, Karl Malden, Jack Nicholson, John Voight, Anthony Perkins ...

Homework: Read the story at home from beginning to end. Be prepared to discuss details.

Unit II
The Meaning of the Title

1. The ending

What actually happens in the story? Give a brief summary.

What had you expected would happen? Did you think that Bogen would be killed?

By McKee? Why?

McKee's 'blood lust' was made very apparent, but some students might have well expected a 'surprise ending'.

Why did McKee shoot Bogen?

If McKee had not killed Bogen, would Tim have shot him?

From appearances only, it could be said (e.g. in a police report or a newspaper story) that Detective McKee was forced to shoot Earl Bogen, when he violently resisted arrest, badly injuring another officer, and was reaching for his weapon. Also, it would appear that Tim would have used his gun (**50** 10–11). His duty, it should be remembered (**49** 13–20), was to cover McKee, that is, to protect him by shooting Bogen if necessary.

2. Tim's motives

Why did Tim lie to Mrs Bogen?

One could take his explanation at face value: **51** 26–32. But one other possible interpretation might need to be argued: Tim lied to Mrs Bogen because he did not want to face the truth about himself. He still wanted to believe that he was different from the other policeman. He would have shot Bogen, after all. His delaying the truth is therefore just like delaying his decision to quit the police force. He cannot face what he is, has become, or will become (a Lt. Mortell).

What was the gift? Who benefited from it?

There are two gifts, each given by Tim. The one he gives the Bogen family is a Christmas not ruined by death (Tim assumes that it is better for her and the family). [The argument that it is cruel or cowardly not to inform Mrs Bogen immediately might also be introduced if it is not raised in class.] The gift he gives himself is the feeling that he has helped in a very small way, if only for a short time, to make an ugly world seem a little bit brighter.

3. Ironic contrasts

What is the effect of the Christmas background on the story?

The Christmas background (as the narrator points out) establishes a feeling of what *should be*, that is, “a tender time”. People should be with their families (instead of on a police stake-out), sharing gifts (instead of exchanging comments on what it is like to kill someone), and enjoying “Silent Night” (instead of hearing shots). Christmas is a time to celebrate “peace on earth” and the birth of a child, and not a time for killing a father of three children. Overall, the Christmas setting provides the author/narrator with an ironic framework, a background upon which to place “wouldn't it be nice, if ...” feelings against the reality of the situation. Tim has to admit that it is not realistic (and would also be a danger to others) to allow Bogen Christmas with his family, for example (**47** 28–33). And Bogen is not just another peaceful citizen carrying packages of warmth and cheer.

4. Alternative endings appropriate to a thriller [Optional]

Do you think the following are as good as/better/worse than the ending actually used?

[As well as being enjoyable, this should be useful in explicating the dramatic structure of “Christmas Gift”. One should also discuss the consequences for the overall effect of the story of any such change in the ending.]

*to follow **50** 9:* Then before I knew what was happening, that other policeman had drawn his gun and its death roared into the no-longer silent night, exploding Bogen's eye into something no-longer human. “Did you have to kill him?” I screamed. McKee was staring at me. Nervously. A frightened kid. “Tim, Tim,” Mortell said, softly. “Poor Tim. You had no choice. He would've killed McKee.”

*to follow **50** 20:* Mrs. Bogen came running up and before I could stop her she had seen his face, or what was left of it, and I had seen hers. “Oh Christ! You've killed him!” she sobbed. “You've killed Father O'Hara!” Just then Dodey and Fischman appeared.

“We got him as he started towards the back yard,” Fischman grunted, and there was Bogen, his face bruised, his hands in the chains, his packages safely in Dodey's big-cop arms. They did look alike, Bogen and 'Hara. Except for the eyes.

“Damn” said Mortell. “There goes Christmas!” As he stood, he stepped on one of the packages. It had once been a baby's rattle.

*to follow **50** 9:* “Oh hell, Thrasher!” Mortell mumbled. He spat on the ground. “You never could shoot worth a damn! You’ve probably blown away some local businessman’s favorite Christmas tree light! That’ll really amuse the Captain, heh?”

McKee had started to giggle. “Step back, kid” Mortell told him. He quickly handcuffed Bogen. He spit on the ground.

Bogen’s face was still terrified. “He — that fat cop” and he looked at Thrasher, “he could have killed me! Me!”

“Yeah, yeah,” Mortell said. “Merry Christmas!”

Homework/Group work suggestion: Write a film script based on this story. To do this, keep all the dialogue and present it as in a play; replace all the narrative with instructions on what is to be filmed and how (long shot, close-up, zoom, fade-out, etc.). Mention special effects, background noises, and music.

Angelica Gibbs

The Test

On the afternoon Marian took her second driver's test, Mrs Ericson went with her. "It's probably better to have someone a little older with you," Mrs Ericson said as Marian slipped into the driver's seat beside her. "Perhaps the last time your Cousin Bill made you nervous, talking too much on the way."

"Yes, Ma'am," Marian said in her soft unaccented voice. "They probably do like it better if a white person shows up with you."

"Oh, I don't think it's *that,*" Mrs Ericson began, and subsided after a glance at the girl's set profile. Marian drove the car slowly through the shady suburban streets. It was one of the first hot days in June, and when they reached the boulevard they found it crowded with cars headed for the beaches.

"Do you want me to drive?" Mrs Ericson asked. "I'll be glad to if you're feeling jumpy." Marian shook her head. Mrs Ericson watched her dark, competent hands and wondered for the thousandth time how the house had ever managed to get along without her, or how she had lived through those earlier years when her household had been presided over by a series of slatternly white girls who had considered housework demeaning and the care of children an added insult. "You drive beautifully, Marian," she said. "Now, don't think of the last time. Anybody would slide on a steep hill on a wet day like that."

"It takes four mistakes to flunk you," Marian said. "I don't remember doing all the things the inspector marked down on my blank."

"People say that they only want you to slip them a little something," Mrs Ericson said doubtfully.

"*No,*" Marian said. "That would only make it worse, Mrs Ericson, I know."

The car turned right, at a traffic signal, into a side road and slid up to the curb at the rear of a short line of parked cars. The inspectors had not arrived yet.

"You have the papers?" Mrs Ericson asked. Marian took them out of her bag: her learner's permit, the car registration, and her birth certificate. They settled down to the dreary business of waiting.

"It will be marvellous to have someone dependable to drive the children to school every day," Mrs Ericson said.

Marian looked up from the list of driving requirements she had been studying. "It'll make things simpler at the house, won't it?" she said.

"Oh, Marian," Mrs Ericson exclaimed, "if I could only pay you half of what you're worth!"

"Now, Mrs Ericson," Marian said firmly. They looked at each other and smiled with affection.

Two cars with official insignia on their doors stopped across the street. The inspectors leaped out, very brisk and military in their neat uniforms. Marian's hands tightened on the wheel. "There's the one who flunked me last time," she whispered, pointing to a stocky, self-important man who had begun to shout directions at the driver at the head of the line. "Oh, Mrs Ericson."

"Now, Marian," Mrs Ericson said. They smiled at each other again, rather weakly.

The inspector who finally reached their car was not the stocky one but a genial, middle-aged man who grinned broadly as he thumbed over their papers. Mrs Ericson started to get out of the car. "Don't you want to come along?" the inspector asked. "Mandy and I don't mind company."

Mrs Ericson was bewildered for a moment. "No," she said, and stepped to the curb. "I might make Marian self-conscious. She's a fine driver, Inspector."

"Sure thing," the inspector said, winking at Mrs Ericson. He slid into the seat beside Marian. "Turn right at the corner, Mandy-Lou."

From the curb, Mrs Ericson watched the car move smoothly up the street.

The inspector made notations in a small black book. "Age?" he inquired presently, as they drove along.

"Twenty-seven."

He looked at Marian out of the corner of his eye. "Old enough to have quite a flock of pickaninnies, eh?"

Marian did not answer.

"Left at this corner," the inspector said, "and park between that truck and the green Buick."

The two cars were very close together, but Marian squeezed in between them without too much maneuvering. "Driven before, Mandy-Lou?" the inspector asked.

"Yes, sir. I had a license for three years in Pennsylvania."

"Why do you want to drive a car?"

"My employer needs me to take her children to and from school."

"Sure you don't really want to sneak out nights to meet some young blood?" the inspector asked. He laughed as Marian shook her head.

"Let's see you take a left at the corner and then turn around in the middle of the next block," the inspector said. He began to whistle "Swanee River." "Make you homesick?" he asked.

Marian put out her hand, swung around neatly in the street, and headed back in the direction from which they had come. "No," she said. "I was born in Scranton, Pennsylvania."

The inspector feigned astonishment. "You-all ain't Southern?" he said. "Well, dog my cats if I didn't think you-all came from down yondah."

"No, sir," Marian said.

"Turn onto Main Street and let's see how you-all does in heavier traffic."

They followed a line of cars along Main Street for several blocks until they came in sight of a concrete bridge which arched high over the railroad tracks.

"Read that sign at the end of the bridge," the inspector said.

"'Proceed with caution. Dangerous in slippery weather,'" Marian said.

"You-all sho can read fine," the inspector exclaimed. "Where d'you learn to do that, Mandy?"

"I got my college degree last year," Marian said. Her voice was not quite steady.

As the car crept up the slope of the bridge the inspector burst out laughing. He laughed so hard he could scarcely give his next direction. "Stop here," he said, wiping his eyes, "then start 'er up again. Mandy got her degree, did she? Dog my cats!"

Marian pulled up beside the curb. She put the car in neutral, pulled on the emergency, waited a moment, and then put the car into gear again. Her face was set. As she released the brake her foot slipped off the clutch pedal and the engine stalled.

"Now, Mistress Mandy," the inspector said, "remember your degree."

"*Damn* you!" Marian cried. She started the car with a jerk.

The inspector lost his joviality in an instant. "Return to the starting place, please," he said, and made four very black crosses at random in the squares on Marian's application blank.

Mrs Ericson was waiting at the curb where they had left her. As Marian stopped the car, the inspector jumped out and brushed past her, his face purple. "What happened?" Mrs Ericson asked, looked after him with alarm.

Marian stared down at the wheel and her lip trembled.

"Oh, Marian, *again*?" Mrs Ericson said.

Marian nodded. “In a sort of different way,” she said, and slid over to the right-hand side of the car.

Biographical Notes

“The Test” was first published in The New Yorker *in 1940. Although the story was widely anthologized in the U.S.A. and Britain, no information can be obtained on the author, nor are any other works by her known to the editors of this collection.*

Annotations

54 6 **Ma’am** [mæm] short for ‘Madam’ (respectful form of address) – **unaccented** without emphasis; in a neutral accent – 7 **to show up** *coll.* to come, to arrive – 8 **to subside** *here:* to become quiet; to stop talking – 9 **set** *here:* with a fixed expression – 11 **to head for** to move towards, to go in the direction of – 14 **jumpy** excited and nervous – 15 **competent** ['–––] able, skilled – 17 **to preside over** to control, to be in charge of – 18 **slatternly** (of women) dirty, careless and untidy – **demeaning** lowering in status, beneath one’s dignity – 19 **insult** ['––] offence to one’s pride – 20 **to slide** to slip on a smooth surface; to skid – 22 **to flunk s.o.** *Am. coll.* to fail s.o. in an exam or test – 23 **blank** form to be filled in – 24 **to slip them ... something** to give them some money secretly – 25 **doubtful** ['daʊtfəl] uncertain – 29 **curb** *Am.* (= *Br.* kerb) edge of footpath – 32 **certificate** [–'–––] official document – 33 **dreary** dull, boring

55 1 **marvellous** ['–––] wonderful – **dependable** [–'–––] that can be trusted – 3 **requirement** s.th. demanded – 7 **firm** strong and sure – 8 **affection** liking – 9 **insignia** [ɪn'sɪgnɪə] emblems – 10 **brisk** quick, active – **neat** tidy – 11 **to tighten** *here:* to hold more firmly – 12 **stocky** short, thick-set – 13 **directions** *here:* instructions – 18 **genial** ['dʒi:nɪəl] friendly, sympathetic – **to thumb over** *here:* to look through quickly, leafing through with one’s thumb – 21 **bewildered** [bɪ'wɪldəd] confused – 22 **self-conscious** nervous and uncomfortable about oneself – 24 **to wink** to close and open one eye quickly – 26 **smoothly** without sudden changes or breaks – 31 **flock** large number (usually of birds or animals) – **pickaninny** (patronizing or derogatory term) Negro child – 34 **Buick** ['bjʊɪk] make of car – 35 **to squeeze in** to force oneself into a small space – 38 **Pennsylvania** U.S. State between Maryland and New York

56 1 **to sneak** to go quietly and secretly – **young blood** *old sl.* handsome young man – 4 **Swanee River** reference to a popular American song about Negroes in the South (first line: "Way down upon de Swanee River, far far away ...") – 9 **to feign** [feɪn] to make a false show of – **astonishment** [-'– – –] great surprise – **you-all** Southern dialect plural form of 'you' (Note that the inspector wrongly uses it as a singular.) – **Southern** from the Southern States, i.e. the former slave-holding States of the U.S. – 10 **dog my cats** *sl.* exclamation of surprise, another attempt to imitate Southern dialect – **yondah = yonder** there (The spelling indicates an attempt to imitate Southern or Black pronunciation, which in this case is similar to British Standard.) – 12 **you-all does** (The 'ungrammatical' verb form is typical of Black English.) – 14 **to arch** to make an upward curve – 17 **to proceed** to move forward – **caution** great care – 18 **sho** = sure (See note on 'yondah' above.) – 20 **college degree** academic title acquired after passing an exam – 21 **steady** sure and even (in tone) – 22 **to creep (crept, crept)** to move slowly – **slope** rising or falling ground – 26 **to pull up** to come to a stop, to stop – **neutral** Leerlauf – **to pull on** to draw one end of s.th. with force – 27 **emergency** *here:* handbrake – **gear** one of the four speeds of a car – 28 **to release** to set free, to unfasten – **clutch** pedal pressed with one's left foot when changing gears – 29 **to stall** [ɔː] to stop suddenly – 32 **joviality** [ˌdʒəʊvɪ'ælɪtɪ] joking manner – **in an instant** at once – 33 **at random** without system – 36 **to brush past** to just touch s.o. as one quickly passes – 37 **purple** dark reddish-blue – 38 **alarm** fear, a feeling of impending disaster – 39 **to tremble** to shake

Interpretation and Teaching Notes

Summary and Analysis

Angelica Gibbs' "The Test" is about the everyday workings of prejudice, and the effect it has on people's lives. In a racially structured society, both the persecuted and the persecutor are aware of the imposed 'rules', which tend to be of the 'heads I win; tails you lose' variety. Members of certain groups are subject to special 'tests' not applicable to others, with special rules of which the outsider is often unaware. Should the victim protest against the unfairness of the rules, he or she is disqualified for having had the presumption to challenge established authority. Should the rules be adhered to, however unwillingly, whatever is thereby gained is tarnished, for it is gained at the cost of self-respect. In short, prejudice imposes a 'no-win' situation on an individual at the outset.

Marian is a 27-year-old, university-educated black woman, born in the North, and employed as a domestic servant. Her duties are considered "demeaning" by less able white girls, but she appears to hold no personal grudge against her well-meaning, if naive employer, Mrs Ericson. Marian needs a driver's license for her job, but she has already failed the test once. The failure may have been partly her own fault, but was more probably the result of an inspector's prejudice (**54** 20–23). Mrs Ericson rides along with Marian on the way to her second test, offering Marian what little moral support she can. Unfortunately, when the (second) inspector is ready to give the (second) test, Mrs Ericson does not accompany them. In not going along, she deprives Marian of a witness to what happens and, in fact, protection from it happening in the first place. Throughout the test, the inspector taunts her with a series of racist and sexist insults thinly disguised as friendly jokes and patronizing goodwill. At first, Marian is able to ignore them, or at least show no reaction. As the insults progress, her self-assurance begins to crumble: she makes a mistake and lets her anger show. As a result, the inspector fails her, marking his grading sheet at random with "four very black crosses". It could be a coincidence, but Marian had four times rejected the inspector's vicious taunts (**56** 2, 7, 11, 31) by refusing to conform to his stereotypes. In other words, she had refused to accept the inspector's definition of her proper role as a black woman, and is being punished for this.

On the surface, Marian fails her driver's test. Equally, she has failed the inspector's racist test (i.e. 'to what extent will she play the game according to my rules?' or 'how badly does she want her license?'). She has also failed her own much more difficult test, that is, not to let herself be provoked.

It is important to notice that what finally destroys Marian's self-control is the ridiculing of her university-degree — the result of intelligence, hard work and considerable determination (especially at a time when women university graduates were not all that common, and black women graduates less so). Prejudice has made a mockery of her university degree: she does not need it for the work available to her, but she does need a driver's license. In effect, the inspector has pointed out with cruel accuracy what she already knows. This is that regardless of her personal achievements and qualities, as a black woman she is totally at the mercy of any white, male petty official who enjoys throwing his weight about.

To fully appreciate the strength of this story it is necessary to also appreciate how extremely crude the inspector is in his racist/sexist taunts, despite the jovial manner in which they are presented. The insulting implications of his direct comments (e.g. **55** 30–31; **56** 12, 45) are unlikely to be overlooked by the reader. They represent a remarkable concentration of the notions held by a certain kind of white male about the proper place of women, blacks, and especially black women. The extremely presumptuous use of name variants may be less obvious. "Mandy" (**55** 20) is not a variant of "Marian" but of "Amanda". By giving her a name he has chosen, the inspector attacks Marian's individuality. Mrs Ericson does lightly 'correct' the inspector, echoing his "Mandy" with her "Marian". Nonetheless, his familiarity along with the sexual overtones of "Mandy and I don't mind company" should have been so obvious that she insisted upon riding along. (But her "bewilderment" (**55** 21) suggests that it is just this suggestion of intimacy which discourages her from going along: she chooses not to annoy the inspector, not to get involved — and thus allows him to dictate his terms to Marian.) "Mandy-Lou" (the caricature of a Southern type name) is equally insulting, but the final mocking variant, "Mistress Mandy" is the worst. It is a form once used by servants (slaves) to their employers (masters), and in the context, extremely sarcastic.

The strength and the depth of "The Test" comes from how quickly and subtly the core of racism is exposed. Marian is not visibly irritated by the most obvious and crudest clichés. Rather, she is provoked by the reminder that ability, educational achievement, and intelligence do not count when the colour of skin determines the choice of tests and the rules for scoring.

Needless to say, the only ones surprised by this situation are those of us who, like Mrs Ericson, are unaware of the 'other' tests and rules, or do not believe that they are really applied. Often, as in Mrs Ericson's case (**54** 8, 20–21) it is a matter of closing one's eyes to the evidence.

Considering how extensively the theme of racial discrimination is now dealt with in literature and the media, students may fail to appreciate the effect this story must have had when it first appeared in 1940. It might be worth pointing out that *The New Yorker* — often castigated as an elitist cultural weekly for the white, liberal establishment (with not a few 'Mrs Ericsons' among its readers) — has an enviable record for initiating debate on controversial topics. Among the influential works which first appeared in *The New Yorker* are John Hersey's *Hiroshima*, Rachel Carson's *Silent Spring* and, more recently, Jonathan Schell's *The Fate of the Earth.* If the situation and the characters in "The Test" seem familiar to students, — especially the racist, foul-mouthed, ill-educated American official – it may be because they have since become stock characters in numerous American films, TV shows, novels, stories and plays.

Unit I
The Exposition: Marian and Mrs Ericson

Preparation: The students could be asked to read the story up to **55** 8 at home. But the approach suggested here functions better if they are confronted with the story for the first time in class.

1. The opening paragraph (read **54** 1–7 in class)
What do you know about Marian and Mrs Ericson at the end of the first seven lines? What can you guess at?
[Concise and rapid entry to the setting, characters and plot is of course one characteristic of the short story. It is not only an economical approach, however. It also has dramatic impact, forcing the reader to actively consider what the setting is, to catch up with the action, and to anticipate what is likely to follow. Gibb's opening "On the afternoon Marian took her second driver's test . . ." is highly effective.
If appropriate to the level of the students, teachers might wish to consider an 'informational' approach. Given incomplete information, the reader is forced to consider probabilities. Once probabilities are considered, they are hypotheses which can be confirmed or denied. Examining the way this applies to the first few lines should sharpen the students' awareness of an important story-telling technique:]

— The first sentence tells us that two women are involved, citizens of an English-speaking country (names and language suggest the U.S.), that Marian is probably younger or lower in social rank than Mrs Ericson (first name as opposed to "Mrs"). We can also assume that Marian had failed her first test (why else have a second?), and that something else might be wrong.
— The second sentence confirms that Mrs Ericson is older, while maintaining the possibility that she is also in some way higher in social ranking.
— The third sentence ("Perhaps ...") allows us to reason that Mrs Ericson and Marian are not, for instance, mother and daughter ("your Cousin Bill" vs. "Cousin Bill"). One also might wonder, as Mrs Ericson talks about someone else talking too much, about her personality.
— The fourth and fifth sentences confirm that Marian is in some socially lower-ranked role with respect to Mrs Ericson ("Ma'am") and make explicit at least part of that relationship: Mrs Ericson is white, and Marian is not white. "Her soft unaccented voice" suggests that she is either somewhat timid and shy, or educated and well-mannered.
— Marian's changing of "someone older" to "a white person" indicates that she does not view the failure in the same way Mrs Ericson does, and that she is not afraid of politely disagreeing with Mrs Ericson.

2. Characterization of Marian and Mrs Ericson (after reading to **55** 8)
How is the picture filled in?
Dialogue confirms what has already been hinted at: the servant/domestic help role; Marian's view as to why she flunked the first test; Mrs Ericson's well-meaning innocence; Marian's mental independence (**54** 26–27, **55** 7), and that the women have some affection for each other, with Marian the more mature or socially aware. The "unaccented voice" topic is also furthered, anticipating Marian's educational background (her speech is grammatical, etc., and Mrs Ericson cannot even pay her half of what she is worth).

3. Reader's expectations
What do you expect to happen? Why?
[It is likely that students will bring in their own experiences, memories of films, etc. as reasons for expecting a certain outcome, in addition to what is given by the story. Some teachers might wish to ask directly if the students are familiar with other stories (films, etc.) which deal with racism or other forms of prejudice, and what their plots were. This could also be a theme for group or written work. Should the students be in general agreement as to what will happen, the teacher might wish to adopt the role of a 'devil's

advocate', and suggest the possibility that Mrs Ericson has already arranged a bribe, or will be present; that Marian will pass the test, but decide to give up her job with Mrs Ericson, etc.]

Homework: Finish the story, and re-read it. Think about explaining why the characters act as they do.

Unit II
The Inspector

1. Comprehension
What did *happen?*
[This question at this point is optional, but (depending upon how students responded to question 3 in Unit I) could serve to clarify any difficulties in understanding the story — and allow those students who "told us so" to tell us so.]

2. The inspector and Mrs Ericson
What does the inspector's first remark tell us?
If we did not know the situation, the inspector's remark (**55** 19–20) could be interpreted as an innocent question: he has nothing against Mrs Ericson accompanying them, and nothing to hide. Likewise, his use of the wrong name, "Mandy", could possibly be a simple mistake. He does deal with many new names and new faces each day. However, as we are aware of the situation, the note of patronizing over-familiarity in his remark tells us that:
— he had perhaps expected Mrs Ericson to want to come along, and is subtly hinting that he might indeed mind;
— he might not be as "genial" (**55** 18) as he first appears;
— Marian might be in a very vulnerable position if Mrs Ericson chooses not to go along.
Why do you think Mrs Ericson was "bewildered for a moment" by the inspector's question? Why did she choose not to come along?
She might have been trying to decide whether the inspector was sincere in asking her to come along, or whether he is subtly hinting that he would rather she didn't. His over-familiarity and the sexual connotations of his remark should have warned her that it might be better for Marian to have someone else in the car. Her stated reason (**55** 22) for not going along is that she might make Marian nervous. This may have been her original intention, but she may now have got the impression that her presence might even

annoy the inspector and cause him to be less benevolent towards Marian. She might still believe — or at least hope — that if someone is a good driver, and the inspector knows this, that person will pass the test. But in effect, she is playing along with the inspector's patronizing attitude towards Marian and expecting Marian to put up with this as well, in order to pass the test. The inspector's "wink" (**55** 24) — which implies complicity — shows that this is the way the inspector sees it.
[Mrs Ericson's choosing not to go along is a turning point in the story; had she been present it is highly unlikely that the inspector would have acted as he did. Had he dared, she would have been a witness. If she (a white, middle-class woman who can afford domestic help) had complained, his job might well have been in danger. The white, liberal 'friend' who would like to help but does not really want to get involved is a familiar figure in black literature.]

3. The inspector's attitude to Marian
What is insulting about the inspector's remarks to Marian?
The first two insults are a mixture of racial and sexual slurs (**55** 30–31, **56** 1–2). They reveal the inspector's racist belief that blacks are driven by primitive sexual urges, and/or his assumption that women can have no serious interest in life except to get a man and have children. After that, the racism is dominant: slavery in the South is hinted at by his "Swanee River" reference (**56** 4) and his parody of black speech (**56** 9). [See also the introductory material on Black English in *Stories from the Black Experience* (Klett). "Swanee River" (1851) by Stephen Forster was associated with ministrel shows in which whites wore 'black face' and ridiculed Negroes and Negro life: these 'blacks' sing words like 'far, far, away ...' from their 'home' in the South, saying in effect that they would rather be there, i.e. that slavery is their natural state.]
The last group of insults (**56** 18–25) deals with Marian's education. It is based on the stereotype of the stupid, illiterate, and uneducated black person. The inspector's final remark ("Mistress Mandy ... remember your degree") combines elements of all the previous insults. There is the patronizing over-familiarity of "Mandy" (see point 2), and the sarcastic use of "Mistress" with its several connotations (old-fashioned form of address for slave-owner or employer of servants — or for a school teacher; it can have a sexual meaning). The mocking reference to Marian's college degree (note that "degree" can also mean a person's station in life) may have reminded Marian that no amount of education can make up for her low social status as a black woman.

Are these remarks deliberate insults?
The inspector no doubt feels that Marian is, in racist terms, an 'uppity nigger' who doesn't know her place. His first few remarks (**55** 30 – **56** 2) may have been thoughtless expressions of his stereotyped view of black people. But he refuses to have this view corrected and becomes deliberately insulting, even when he hears that Marian is college-educated. It should be noted that the inspector only begins his parody of black speech after he knows that Marian is not from the South (**56** 9).

4. Marian's reactions to the inspector
How does Marian react to these insults? Try to explain her reactions.
She ignores the first remark, and just shakes her head in response to the mocking question about her reasons for wanting a driver's license. She is probably used to such taunts from white people and has found that ignoring them and remaining calm is the only way to survive.
By her explicit statement that she is not from the South she probably hopes to put an end to one particular kind of taunt — but does not succeed, since the inspector does not seem to be interested in facts (**56** 9).
The next insult affects her more visibly (**56** 20–21) — either because she now sees that this is a game she just cannot win, or because she is more sensitive to insults which make a mockery of her intelligence and education.
The final insult, which is brought on by a mistake caused by her growing nervousness and irritation (**56** 27–30), is the last straw, as it were.

5. The meaning of the title
What "test" did Marian fail?
Obviously, she failed her driver's test. But since it wasn't because of a lack of driving skill, one could say that she failed this particular inspector's test of her behaviour: she failed to conform to his definition of a black woman's proper role. She also failed her own test — to keep cool under pressure.
What do you think Marian means when she says she failed "In a sort of different way"?
Earlier in the story (**54** 22–23), Marian hinted that she suspected prejudice as the reason for failing the first test. But she had presumably behaved politely, ignoring any insults and still not passed. It is not clear whether or not Marian would have passed the test the second time if she had kept her cool and avoided swearing at the inspector. But certainly the series of insults had reached the point where the license was not worth her self-respect.
What else is 'tested' by the situation described in the story?
In a way, Marian's driving test is also a test of social justice and of equal

rights for black and white, men and women. And if this is regarded as a 'test case', then society fails miserably. In effect, the story amounts to a strong indictment of social injustice.

Homework/Group work suggestions:

1. If it is thought useful to try to separate the racist from the sexist elements in the inspector's behaviour, it could be discussed how he might have behaved towards a black man — or a white woman.

2. Prejudice can often be expressed in very subtle ways — the speaker (or writer) may not even be aware of being prejudiced, but unthinkingly apply different standards to different groups of people. Students might collect examples of prejudiced language from magazines, newspaper articles and even schoolbooks, discuss their implications and suggest what an individual can do to counteract such tendencies. Some common examples: using a phrase like "black athlete" in sports stories when a white person's race is not considered relevant; referring to the physical characteristics of women only, e.g. "attractive young lawyer", "blond, blue-eyed ...".

3. There are a large numbers of stories and tales from all cultures and periods in which a hero is repeatedly tested by a succession of monsters, tragedies, tortures, etc. The plot in fact is one of the best-known folktale types. In each case, the hero can only win if he/she does not lose faith, show anger, deny friends, etc. Students might be asked to select any story reflecting this theme (e.g. the fairy tale in this collection) and compare it with "The Test".

Dal Stivens

The Pepper-Tree

My father often spoke about the pepper-tree when we were kids, and it was clear it meant a lot to him. It stood for something – like the Rolls-Royce he was always going to buy. It wasn't what he said about the pepper-tree – my father had no great gift for words – but how he said it that counted. When he spoke of the pepper-tree at Tullama where he had been brought up you saw it clearly; a monster of a tree with long shawls of olive-green leaves in a big generous country-town backyard. "A decent backyard – none of your city pocket-handkerchief lots," my father said. There were berries on the tree that turned from green to pink with waxlike covers which you could unpick and get the sticky smell of them all over your fingers. In this spanking tree there was always, too, a noisy traffic of sparrows and starlings fluttering and hopping from branch to branch.

When we lived at Newtown, Sydney, I used to look for pepper-trees when my father took me for a walk on Sunday afternoons. "Look, there's a pepper-tree," I'd say to him when I saw one with its herring-bone leaves.

"By golly, boy, that's only a little runt of a tree," my old man would say. "They don't do so well in the city. Too much smoke, by golly. You ought to see them out west where I come from."

My father was a tall, thin man with melancholy brown eyes and the soul of a poet. It was the poet in him that wanted to own a Rolls-Royce one day.

"First our own house and then some day, when my ship comes home, I'll buy a Rolls-Royce," he'd say.

Some of his friends thought my old man was a little crazy to have such an ambition.

"What would you do with one of those flash cars, Peter?" they'd tease him. "Go and live among the swells?"

My father would stroke his long brown moustache, which had only a few bits of white in it, and try to explain, but he couldn't make them understand. He couldn't even get his ideas across to my mother. Only now do I think I understand what a Rolls-Royce meant to him.

"I don't want to swank it, as you put it, Emily," he'd say to my mother. "No, by golly. I want to own a Rolls-Royce because it is the most perfect piece of machinery made in this world. Why, a Rolls-Royce –"

And then he'd stop and you could feel him groping for the right words to describe what he felt, and then go on blunderingly with the caress of a lover in his voice, talking about how beautiful the engine was. . . .

"What would a garage mechanic do with a Rolls-Royce, I ask you!" my mother would say. "I'd feel silly sitting up in it."

At such times my mother would give the wood stove in the kitchen a good shove with the poker, or swish her broom vigorously. My mother was a small plump woman with brown hair which she wore drawn tight back from her forehead.

Like the pepper-tree, the Rolls-Royce symbolized something for my father. He had been born in Tullama in the mallee. His father was a bricklayer and wanted his son to follow him. But my father had had his mind set on becoming an engineer. When he was eighteen he had left Tullama and come to the city and got himself apprenticed to a mechanical engineer. He went to technical classes in the evening. After two years his eyes had given out on him.

"If I had had some money things might have been different, by golly," my father told me once. "I could have gone to the university and learnt things properly. I could have become a civil engineer. I didn't give my eyes a fair go – I went to classes five nights a week and studied after I came home."

After his eyes went, my father had to take unskilled jobs but always near machinery. "I like tinkering but I had no proper schooling," he said once.

He knew a lot and in spite of his eyes he could only have learnt most of it from books. He knew all about rocks and how they were formed. He could talk for hours, if you got him started, about fossils and the story of evolution. My mother didn't like to hear him talking about such things because she thought such talk was irreligious. Looking back now I'd say that in spite of his lack of orthodox schooling my father was a learned man. He taught me more than all the teachers I ever had at high school. He was a keen naturalist, too.

Just before the depression came when we were living at Newtown, my father had paid one hundred pounds off the house. He was forty-seven years old then. I was twelve.

"By golly, we'll own the house before we know where we are," he said.

"Will we?" said my mother. "At a pound a week we have twelve years to go – unless we win Tatts."

"You never know what may turn up," said my old man cheerfully.

"I have a good idea what with people losing their jobs every day."

"I haven't lost mine," my father said, "and what's more, if I do, I have a way of making some money."

"I suppose it's another of your inventions, Peter? What is it this time, I ask you?"

"Never you mind," said my father. But he said it gently.

One of my mother's complaints was that my father was always losing money on the things he tried to invent. Another was that he was always filling the backyard up with junk.

"What can you do with these pocket-handkerchief lots?" my father would say. "Now, when I was a nipper at Tullama we had a decent backyard – why it was immense – it was as big –"

He'd stop there not being able to get the right word.

Auction sales, according to my mother, were one of my father's weaknesses. He could never resist anything if it looked cheap, even if he had no use for it, she'd say. Soon after my old man had told my mother he had something in mind to make some money, he went away early one Sunday morning. He came back about lunch-time in a motor lorry. On the back of the Ford was a two-stroke kerosene engine. I came running out.

"I've bought it, Joe, by golly," he told me.

He had, too. Both engine and lorry.

"Dirt cheap. Forty quid the lot," he said. "Ten quid down, boy, and ten bob a week."

My mother cut up when she heard.

"Wasting money when it could have gone into the house, Peter."

"This'll pay the house off in no time, by golly," my father said. "And buy a lot of other things, too."

I knew by the way he looked up and over my mother's head he was thinking of the Rolls-Royce which to him was like a fine poem or a great symphony of Beethoven.

All that day he was very excited, walking round the engine, standing back to admire it, and then peering closely at it. He started it running and stopped it continually all the afternoon. Every night when he came home from the garage during the next week, he'd go first thing and look at the engine. He had some plan in his mind but wouldn't say what it was at first.

"Wait and see, Joe," he'd said. "You'll see all right."

He didn't let me into his secret for over a week, although I knew he was bursting to tell someone. In the end, he drew me aside mysteriously in the kitchen one night, when my mother was in the bedroom, and whispered, "It's an invention for cleaning out underground wells, boy."

"For cleaning out wells?"

"Underground wells."

He listened to hear if my mother was coming back.

"I'm rigging a light out there tonight, boy," he whispered. "Come out later and I'll show you."

My father's idea, he explained later, was to clean underground wells in country towns by suction. You pushed a stiff brush on the end of the pipe down the sides and along the bottom of underground wells. The pipe sucked up the silt and you didn't lose much water from the well.

"Every country town has half a dozen underground wells, boy," he said. "The banks and one or two of the wealthier blokes in the town. Just like it was in Tullama. There's money in it because you can clean the well out without losing too much water. It's a gold-mine."

It sounded good to me.

"When do you start?" I asked.

"Soon, by golly," he said. "The job at the garage won't spin out much longer."

He was right about that, but until the day she died my mother always had a sneaking idea that the old man had helped to give himself the sack. It was early in 1930 when the old man set out in the lorry, heading out west.

"You've got to go to the low-rainfall districts," he said.

"Like Tullama?" I said.

"Yes, like Tullama, by golly."

I started thinking of the pepper-tree then.

"Will you go to Tullama and see the pepper-tree?"

My father stroked his long straggling moustache. Into his eyes came that look like when he was thinking or talking about the Rolls. He didn't answer me for a bit.

"By golly, yes, boy, if I go there."

Soon after this he started off. Every week brought a letter from him. He did well too. He was heading almost due west from Sydney and I followed the towns he spoke of in my school atlas. It took him nearly a day on a well, so in the larger towns he might stay over a week, in the smaller a day or a day and a half.

After he had been away for two months he still had a good few wells to go before he reached Tullama. You could see that he was heading that way.

"Him and that silly pepper-tree!" said my mother, but she didn't say it angrily. My father was sending her as much money as he used to bring home when he worked at the garage.

But in spite of what my mother said about the pepper-tree, she became a bit keen as my father got only two weeks off Tullama. She made a small pin-flag for me to stick on the map. About this time a change came in the old man's letters home. At first they had been elated, but now they were quieter. He didn't boast so much about the money he was making, or say anything about the Rolls. Perhaps excitement was making him quieter as he got nearer to the pepper-tree, I thought.

"I know what it is," my mother said. "He's not getting his proper meals. He's too old to be gallivanting off on his own. I bet he's not cooking proper meals for himself. And without a decent bed to sleep in – only the back of that lorry."

I thought the day would never come, but soon enough my dad had only one town to do before he would reach Tullama. His letters usually arrived on a Tuesday – he wrote home on the Sundays – but round this time I watched for the mail every day and was late for school three mornings running. When a letter did come I grabbed it from the postman's hand and hurried inside with it, reading the post-mark on the run. It was from Tullama.

"All right, all right, don't rush me, Joe," my mother said. "You and your pepper-tree."

I read over her elbow. There was only one page. There was nothing about the pepper-tree. Dad was well and making money, but he was thinking of returning soon. Only a few lines.

I couldn't understand it.

On the next Tuesday there was no letter. Nor on the Wednesday. On the Thursday my father came home. He turned up at breakfast-time. He gave us a surprise walking in like that. He said that he had sold the truck and engine and come home by train. He looked tired and shamefaced and somehow a lot older. I saw a lot more white in his moustache.

"The engine was no good," he said. "It kept breaking down. It cost me nearly all I earned and it was hungry on petrol. I had to sell it to pay back what I borrowed and get my fare home."

"Oh, Peter," my mother said, putting her arms round him. "You poor darling. I knew something was wrong."

"Mother reckoned it was the food," I said. "She reckoned you weren't getting your proper meals."

"I'll make you a cup of tea, Peter," my mother said, bustling over to the stove and pushing another piece of wood into it. "Then I'll get you some breakfast."

"By golly, that sounds a bit of all right," my father said then. This was the first time since he had walked in that he had sounded like his old self.

My mother hurried about the kitchen and my father talked a bit more. "I thought I was going to do well at first," he said. "But the engine was too old. It was always spare parts. It ate up all I earned."

He talked on about the trip. I had got over my surprise at seeing him walk in and now wanted to know all about the pepper-tree.

"Did you see the pepper-tree, dad?"

"Yes, I saw it all right."

I stood directly in front of him as he sat at the table, but he was not looking at me but at something far away. He didn't answer for what seemed a long time.

"It was a little runt of a tree, boy – and a little backyard."

He wouldn't say any more than that and he never spoke of the pepper-tree – or the Rolls – again.

Biographical Notes

Dallas George Stivens, a fifth-generation Australian, was born in New South Wales in 1911 and was educated in Sydney. During World War II he joined the Australian Army Education Service and afterwards worked in the Australian Department of Information.

Dal Stivens is best known for his satirical novel Jimmy Brockett, *which was first published in 1951. A number of other novels, and several collections of short stories followed in the fifties and sixties. Dal Stivens was a recipient of the Commonwealth Literary Fund Fellowship in 1951, 1962 and 1970. Commenting on his own work, he says his "underlying interest has been in the tension between illusion and reality, art and life". This is something which comes out clearly in our story. Dal Stivens is married and has two children.*

Annotations

59 **pepper-tree** subtropical evergreen tree with bright red fruit – 4 **gift** *here:* talent – 5 **Tullama** probably Tullamore, a small town in New South Wales – 7 **generous** *here:* with lots of space – **decent** ['di:sənt] *coll.* proper, as it should be; of the right size – 8 **lot** area of land (Parzelle) – 10 **to unpick** to take out from – **spanking** *coll.* fine, excellent – 11 **sparrow** common small brownish bird (Sperling) – **starling** common greenish-black bird (Star) – 12 **to flutter** (of birds) to move the wings quickly – 16 **by golly** *Austr. sl.* expression of surprise (= by God) – **runt** an underdeveloped specimen – 17 **don't do so well** don't grow so well – 19 **melancholy** ['– – – –] sad – 24 **ambition** strong desire (for success, etc.) – 25 **flash** *coll.* costly-looking – **to tease** to make fun of – 26 **the swells** *sl.* rich and elegant people – 27 **to stroke** to rub gently – 29 **to get s.th. across** *coll.* to make o.s. understood – 31 **to swank it** *coll.* to show off – **as you put it** as you say

60 1 **to grope for** to search for uncertainly – 2 **to blunder** *here:* to express one's thoughts or feelings in an awkward manner – **caress** [kə'res] gesture expressing love – 7 **shove** [ʃʌv] heavy push – **poker** long metal stick for stirring a fire – **to swish** to move s.th. (through the air) with a sharp whistling sound – **broom** long-handled sweeping brush (Besen) – **vigorous** ['vɪgərəs] strong – 9 **forehead** ['fɒrɪd] part of the face above the eyes – 11 **in the mallee** ['mæli:] in the bush; out in the eucalyptus forests – **bricklayer** person who builds walls and houses with bricks – 12 **to set one's mind on** to want very much – 14 **to get o.s. apprenticed to s.o.** to start training in a particular skill – 15 **to give out** *coll.* to lose, to break down – 19 **civil engineer** engineer responsible for planning, building and repairing public works (Bauingenieur) – **a fair go** a fair chance – 21 **after his eyes went** after his eyesight became bad – **unskilled jobs** jobs for untrained workers – 22 **to tinker** to play around with (machines) – 28 **orthodox** proper, conventional – **learned** ['lɜ:nɪd] having very much knowledge – 24 **keen** very interested, enthusiastic – 30 **naturalist** person who studies plants and animals – 31 **depression** economic crisis with high unemployment – 32 **to pay ... off the house** to pay back some of the debt on the house – 36 **Tatts** an Australian lottery – 38 **what with** considering

61 3 **never you mind** that's none of your business – 6 **junk** *coll.* old things of little or no value – 8 **nipper** *Austr. coll.* small child – 12 **to resist s.th.** *here:* to keep away from – 16 **two-stroke engine** Zweitaktmotor – **kerosene** oil distilled from petroleum – 19 **dirt cheap** *coll.* very cheap – **quid** *sl.* a pound (£ 1); *here:* Australian pound (nowadays, the monetary unit of Australia is the dollar) – **the lot** number of articles sold (or bought) together – **ten quid down** £ 10 in cash – 20 **bob** *coll.* shilling (now 5p) – 21 **to cut up** *coll.* to be very upset or angry – 29 **to admire** *here:* to look at with pleasure – **to peer** to look carefully – 30 **continually** over and over again – 35 **bursting to do s.th.** wanting very much to do s.th.; waiting for an opportunity – 37 **well** hole drilled into the earth to get water

62 1 **to rig s.th.** to construct, to put up – 4 **suction** act of sucking (Saugwirkung) – **stiff** not easily movable; not flexible – 6 **silt** loose sand, mud – 8 **bloke** *sl.* fellow, man – 13 **to spin out** *here:* to last, to continue – 16 **sneaking** vague, not clearly or openly expressed – **to give s.o. the sack** to dismiss (from a job), to fire – 23 **straggling** spread untidily – 28 **to head** to move in a certain direction – **due west** directly west – 40 **elated** filled with pride and joy

63 1 **to boast** to talk proudly – 5 **to gallivant** [,––'–] *coll.* to travel around, to go off amusing o.s. – **on one's own** alone – 11 **three mornings running** . . . one after another, in a row – 12 **to grab** to snatch, to take in one's hand quickly – 13 **on the run** *here:* while hurrying – 22 **to turn up** to arrive – 24 **shamefaced** looking as if one is ashamed of s.th. – 33 **to bustle** ['bʌsl] to appear to be very busy – 36 **a bit of all right** *sl.* fine, great – 40 **spare parts** Ersatzteile – **it was always ...** *here:* it always needed . . . – **to eat up** *here:* to use up

Interpretation and Teaching Notes

Summary and Analysis

As the title indicates, this story is set in a sub-tropical country. In fact it has an Australian background. Recollecting his childhood days in a Sydney suburb, the narrator draws a portrait of his father, a tall, thin, melancholy man with "the soul of a poet" (**59** 19–20).

As a bricklayer's son from the country town of Tullama, his father had come to Sydney at the age of eighteen in the hope of becoming a civil engineer. His studies at evening classes, however, began to strain his eyesight, so that his plans came to nothing. Nevertheless, as a plain garage mechanic he set his mind on inventing things and — as his wife saw it – began to fill their small backyard up with junk.

Feeling cramped on the small suburban lot and regretting his lack of proper education, he would tell his son about the unmatched splendour of a certain pepper-tree back home at Tullama. At the same time he started dreaming of being the owner of a Rolls-Royce one day — in his eyes, "the most perfect piece of machinery made in this world" (**59** 32–33).

One Sunday he came home from an auction with a two-stroke kerosene engine on the back of a lorry. For over a week he could be seen tinkering with the engine after work. Finally, one night he informed his then 12-year-old son that he had invented a machine for cleaning out underground wells. In view of the Australian dependence on such wells for their water supply and for irrigation, he expected it to be "a gold mine" (**62** 10).

Early in 1930 he quit his job at the garage and set out for the low-rainfall districts in the west. He also took up his son's suggestion that he should go and see the pepper-tree at Tullama on his tour. For two months the boy and his mother received a weekly letter from him, with money enclosed. They began following his route in the boy's school atlas and saw that he was obviously heading for Tullama. But when the postman finally delivered a letter from Tullama, to the boy's dismay it said nothing about the pepper-tree, but briefly announced his father's intention of returning.

When his father came home, "tired and shamefaced and somehow a lot older" (**63** 24–25), he had to admit that he had given up on his invention, which had proved uneconomic. The pepper-tree at Tullama, it turned out, had been "a little runt of a tree" in "a little backyard" (**64** 8). Neither the pepper-tree nor the Rolls were ever mentioned again.

What makes this narrative so interesting to read or listen to is the fact that it contains two stories in one: the pathetic tale of a man's failure to realize his ambitions, and the story of his son's disappointment in him. What welds these two stories into one convincing whole is the narrator's adult insights (cf. **59** 1–2, 29–30). He seldom tells us directly what these insights are (some tentative suggestions: **59** 19–20, **60** 27–28). But the way he presents his childhood memories, stressing and combining particular details, gives us a good chance of reaching the same level of understanding as he has himself.

In retrospect, the son probably realizes that the father's glorified memory of the pepper-tree of his youth as well as his dreams of owning a Rolls-Royce were nothing but attempts to flee from his unsatisfactory existence as a plain garage mechanic who once had yearned to be a civil engineer.

When the sight of the "little runt of a tree" in Tullama proves beyond a shadow of doubt that the former was an illusion, he loses faith in his grandiose hopes for the future. Of course, the technical problems of his invention might be sufficient to explain the father's defeat at the end of the story. But technical (and health and money) problems had been overcome before, with the help of his dream. Now that his illusions are gone, there is nothing left to sustain him.

Even at the time, the narrator seems to have been fully aware of his father's double failure. He neither succeeded with his hopeful invention nor could he corroborate his exciting picture of the pepper-tree once he had kindled the child's imagination with his vivid reports. It must have been a considerable disappointment for the boy to have his innocent belief in the power of his father's judgement destroyed. But there is no condemnation, no scorn. Everywhere a spirit of understanding permeates through the narrative, and an awareness of his father's human qualities: his overflowing imagination, his love of nature, his zeal for knowledge, his confidentiality towards his son, and — above all — a certain poetic quality which was sadly thwarted by the circumstances of his life.

Unit I
The Father and His Dreams (Listening Comprehension)

Introductory Remarks:

— The following unit can be based either on the recording (Klettnummer 57737) or on a first reading of the story in class. If so desired, the students can be asked to read the story (to **62** 26) at home and the questions then adapted accordingly.

— Before playing the recording, it might be advisable to prepare the students for the unaccustomed accent of the speaker. It should suffice to point out that the "pepper-tree" of the title is a sub-tropical tree, and that the writer is himself an Australian. If — after listening to the recording — the teacher wishes to go into detail about the accent, the main deviations from British standard pronunciation are listed on page 181.

1. Play the recording, covering the text from page **59** 1 to page **62** 26. Clarify any language difficulties. Replay this extract.

2. Comprehension questions
Who is telling the story?
How old is he when he is telling the story?
How old was he at the time?
The narrator is a person called Joe, now an adult. It is a recollection of his childhood days at Newton, Sydney in the late 1920s and early 1930s, when he was about twelve years old (**59** 1, 13; **60** 31, 33; **62** 17).
What is the main subject of this extract?
What kind of information does the narrator give us? In what order?
The narrator focuses on his impressions of his father, then a forty-seven-year-old garage mechanic (**59** 25; **60** 4, 32–33). He tells us about conversations he used to have with his father, and what his mother and the neighbours used to say. All this is pieced together from various episodes in his childhood and interspersed with generalizations (e.g. **59** 19–20). One could refer to this as an extended exposition. Only when the main episode starts does the narrative become chronological (from **61** 13 on).
What do we learn about the father's past?
Joe's father was obviously a person to whom life was not particularly kind. He was a bricklayer's son who at the age of 18 left his home town of Tullama for Sydney in the hope of becoming an engineer one day. There he got himself apprenticed to a mechanical engineer and went to evening classes. However, his dreams were shattered pretty soon because of his bad eyesight and his lack of money (**60** 11–16).
His lack of proper schooling forced him to take unskilled jobs (**60** 21) to support his family and pay off the debt on their little house (**59** 21, **60** 31–36).
What do you learn about the father's dreams and ambitions?
What did his family and friends think of such dreams?

His dream of becoming a civil engineer had come to nothing due to adverse circumstances (see above). At the time the narrator remembers, his father was left with two ambitions (**59** 21–22). He was well on the way to realizing the first — his hope of one day owning the house they lived in. But it would be some time before he had paid off the debt, and his wife was worried in case he might lose his job in the depression before then (**60** 31–40). His second remaining dream was laughed at by everybody (**59** 23–29, **60** 4–5): he wanted to own a Rolls-Royce one day. To his wife and the neighbours, this ambition was totally inappropriate for a garage mechanic, so they would tease him and scoff at him for his apparent delusions of grandeur and desire for social climbing.

Why did he say he wanted to own a Rolls-Royce?

Whenever anybody asked him, he would talk about a Rolls as being "the most perfect piece of machinery made in this world" (**59** 32–33). But he found it hard to express his feelings clearly, so nobody could understand why he should want to own one. The narrator tells us that he later came to understand that the Rolls-Royce "symbolized something" for his father (**59** 2–3, 29–30; **60** 10–11).

What was the father's money-making scheme?

Was it only the need for money that made him take it up?

He had always liked tinkering with machines and inventing things, and now he managed to construct a machine for cleaning out underground wells. When he finally lost his job, he set off around the country offering this service to the rich owners of such wells. His wife suspected that he had deliberately got himself sacked; and one definitely gets the impression that he enjoyed doing this kind of work a lot more than his job at the garage.

Homework: Read the whole story, to find out what became of the father's scheme and to make sure you have understood all the details.

Unit II
Pepper-Tree and Rolls-Royce: Symbols of Something

1. The ending

How does the story end? What is stressed in the last line?

It ends with the boy's father admitting defeat. His machine is a failure, technically and financially. He also finds out that the pepper-tree at Tullama is just as small as those in the city, and nothing like what he thought he remembered. After that he gives up his project and comes home. The last line tells that he also gives up fantasizing about the tree and the Rolls-Royce.

Suggested blackboard sketch for points 2 and 3:
Situation at time of father's money-making scheme

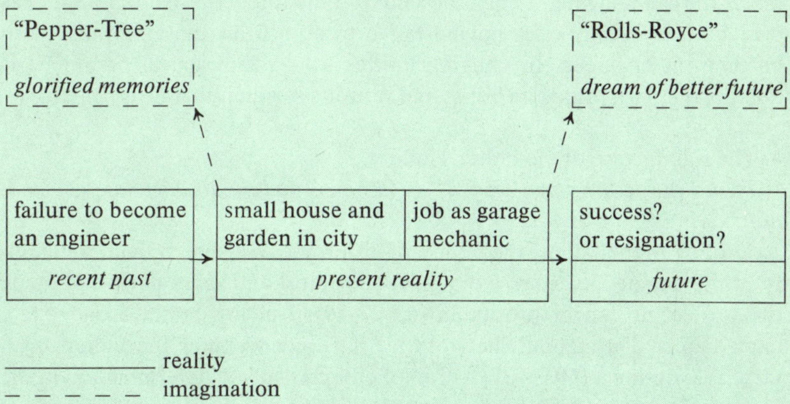

2. The significance of the pepper-tree
Why do you think the father talked so much about the pepper-tree at Tullama?
The father really seems to have believed that the pepper-tree at Tullama was much bigger and better than any he had seen in the city. Whenever he mentions it, he contrasts it with some unfavourable aspect of city life (**59** 8, 17). In a way it comes to stand for better times in the past, in the country.
Unlike the city, whose stifling living-conditions are frequently referred to, the pepper-tree is presented as an idyll in the true sense of the word. The tree at Tullama — as the father remembers it — gratified the senses in almost every respect. The tree's berries could be picked, touched and smelled; its foliage was full of noisy "fluttering and hopping" birds (**59** 6–12). Such talk signals his inner flight from his drab existence in the big city, the place which witnessed his defeat in early manhood.

3. The significance of the Rolls-Royce
How would you explain the father's wish to own a Rolls-Royce?
While the pepper-tree stands for the father's memories of better times in the

past, the luxurious car seems to stand for his hope for a better future. The idea of owning a Rolls seems to sum up several hidden wishes. The obvious one is the desire for social success and riches. He strongly denies that he wants "to swank it" (**59** 31), but there is probably some link in his mind between the Rolls and the idea of escaping from his working-class existence and constant money worries. The other one is what he says himself (and there is no reason to doubt his sincerity): a longing for the beauty and perfection represented by the Rolls. Since it is the best thing a garage mechanic can imagine, it might be said to stand for all the aspirations he has ever had, especially after having failed to realize his first ambition — to become an engineer. In clinging to this totally impractical dream he is holding on to his pride and hope, and refusing to admit that he is beaten.

4. The significance of the father's failure

Why did the father's project fail? Is technical failure an adequate explanation?

According to the father, the failure of his project was due to the unreliability of the engine. Its excessive hunger for petrol and spare parts had made the project no longer profitable (**63** 27–40). But this is not an adequate explanation. Throughout the story we have got to know the father as an incurable optimist (**60** 34–37) — full of enthusiasm and determination in the face of adversity (**60** 12–13), making the best of his situation and his limited means (**60** 13–15, 20, 23–30), and always finding ways of explaining away his failures and coming up with new reasons to go on trying (**60** 17–19, 39–40; **61** 23–24). It seems a bit out of character for him to give up so completely on his invention, which after all, worked very well for a while (**62** 35–36), and whose failure to make a profit was easily attributable to the shortcomings of the second-hand engine it was based on. Note that he could probably have kept going for a while: when he says "It ate up all I earned" (**63** 40) he seems to be exaggerating a bit — a few lines before he had said "It cost me *nearly* all I earned".

What could have changed his attitude?

What is the first sign of such a change?

The first sign of change is in his letters home as he approaches Tullama (**62** 39 – **63** 3). He had obviously taken up the boy's suggestion enthusiastically (**62** 22–26, 33) and was heading towards his home town in the hope of having his memory of the magnificent tree confirmed. The boy's conjecture that "excitement was making him quieter" (**63** 2) may be quite correct. The absence of any reference to the tree in his letter from Tullama shows that something is very wrong. As it turns out, the tree was nothing like what the father thought he remembered, but "a little runt of a tree" just like those in the city, in "a little backyard" (**64** 8). This disillusionment affects him deeply: now that he sees how unrealistic his nostalgic dreams of youth in the country were, he loses faith in his dreams of a better future (as symbolized by the Rolls) and never speaks of either again (**64** 9–10).

Homework: Write a short note summing up what the pepper-tree "stood for" (**59** 2) and what the Rolls-Royce "symbolized" (**60** 10) for the boy's father.

Unit III
The Narrator's Perspective — Then and Now

1. Narrator and central character
Whose story is it?
At first sight, it seems of course to be the father's story — the story of his struggles in the past and his shattered dreams. Nonetheless, the perspective from which the story is told makes it clear that it is also the narrator's story. The father's nostalgic praise of the pepper-tree at Tullama had kindled his son's childish imagination to the extent that he began to identify the success of his father's tour with his corroboration of the splendour of the tree (**62** 22; **63** 3–4, 8–20; **64** 1–2). Consequently, the father's failure disillusioned both persons alike. At the end of the story both had to bid good-bye to their dreams: the father from his romanticized picture of his juvenile past and his belief in a better future; the narrator, then a child, from his innocent trust in his father's infallibility.

2. The 'child's eye' view
What are we told about the young boys' feelings about his father?
Most of the narrative is a relatively neutral account of what the father used to say and do, and what people used to say of him. But here and there the narrator lets us know how much of an impression his father made on him. His talk of the pepper-tree stimulated the boy's imagination (**59** 4–7); he liked to get him talking about geology and natural history (**60** 24–26); and he seems to have had a better imaginative or intuitive understanding of his father's feelings than his mother had (**60** 1–2, 4–9, 26–27; **61** 25–27). It is clear that father and son were very fond of each other (**61** 34–**62** 26), so the boy must have been deeply upset by his father's failure.

3. Narrative distance: the adult looking back

What makes it clear that the narrator is now grown up?

A number of phrases make it clear that he is looking back on his childhood days (**59** 1, 29; **60** 26). There are also a number of comparisons that are obviously not the thoughts of a child (**59** 19–20, **60** 26–27).

In what light does he see the episode now?

A number of comments indicate that the narrator does not want his story to be misinterpreted as a sort of belated protest. The psychological significance which the pepper-tree and the Rolls used to have for his father is mentioned right at the beginning of the story and reconfirmed several times (**59** 1–3, 20, 29–30; **60** 1–3, 10). Though he says he now understands things better (**59** 29–30) he does not go into too much detail about his interpretation, but tells the story in such a way that we can reach a similar understanding ourselves. He points out the social background of his father (**60** 11–22, 31–32). He puts a lot of emphasis on the attractive sides of his father's character: his overflowing imagination (**59** 4–12), his love of nature and his zeal for knowledge (**60** 23–30), his confidentiality toward his son (**61** 34–37), his tenderness towards his uncomprehending wife (**61** 3, **63** 36). This sympathetic view of the father makes the subsequent account of his defeat appear in a tragic light — not because the little boy felt let down, but because he now understands what it must have meant to his father to say goodbye to his dreams.

4. Comparison with Shirley Jackson's story "Charles" [if already read and discussed]

What is similar about the point of view in "Charles"?

Both stories are told by a first-person narrator, both focus on another member of the family, and both events are viewed in retrospect. In addition, it is very relevant in each case that the events related were not fully understood at the time they happened — the understanding came later. But the effect of this 'double vision' is completely different: in "Charles", the effect is comic, in "The Pepper-Tree" it is almost tragic.

Which of the two stories did you enjoy reading most? Why?
Which would you enjoy reading again?
Which story gives you more to think about?
Would you say one is better than the other? Why?

William Saroyan

The Great Leapfrog Contest

Rosie Mahoney was a tough little Irish kid whose folks, through some miscalculation in directions, or out of an innate spirit of anarchy, had moved into the Russian-Italian-and-Greek neighborhood of my home town, across the Southern Pacific tracks, around G Street.

She wore a turtle-neck sweater, usually red. Her father was a bricklayer named Cull and a heavy drinker. Her mother's name was Mary. Mary Mahoney used to go to the Greek Orthodox Catholic Church on Kearny Boulevard every Sunday, because there was no Irish Church to go to anywhere in the neighborhood. The family seemed to be a happy one.

Rosie's three brothers had all grown up and gone to sea. Her two sisters had married. Rosie was the last of the clan. She had entered the world when her father had been close to sixty and her mother in her early fifties. For all that, she was hardly the studious or scholarly type.

Rosie had little use for girls, and as far as possible avoided them. She had less use for boys, but found it undesirable to avoid them. That is to say, she made it a point to take part in everything the boys did. She was always on hand, and always the first to take up any daring or crazy idea. Everybody felt awkward about her continuous presence, but it was no use trying to chase her away, because that meant a fight in which she asked no quarter, and gave none.

If she didn't whip every boy she fought, every fight was at least an honest draw, with a slight edge in Rosie's favor. She didn't fight girl-style, or cry if hurt. She fought the regular style and took advantage of every opening. It was very humiliating to be hurt by Rosie, so after a while any boy who thought of trying to chase her away, decided not to.

It was no use. She just wouldn't go. She didn't seem to like any of the boys especially, but she liked being in on any mischief they might have in mind, and she wanted to play on any teams they organized. She was an excellent baseball player, being as good as anybody else in the neighborhood at any position, and for her age an expert pitcher. She had a wicked wing, too, and could throw a ball in from left field that when it hit the catcher's mitt it made a nice sound.

She was extraordinarily swift on her feet and played a beautiful game of tin-can hockey.

At pee-wee, she seemed to have the most disgusting luck in the world.

At the game we invented and used to call *Horse* she was as good at *horse* as at *rider,* and she insisted on following the rules of the game. She insisted on being horse when it was her turn to be horse. This always embarrassed her partner, whoever he happened to be, because it didn't seem right for a boy to be getting up on the back of a girl.

She was an excellent football player too.

As a matter of fact, she was just naturally the equal of any boy in the neighborhood, and much the superior of many of them. Especially after she had lived in the neighborhood three years. It took her that long to make everybody understand that she had come to stay and that she was *going* to stay.

She did, too; even after the arrival of a boy named Rex Folger, who was from somewhere in the south of Texas. This boy Rex was a natural-born leader. Two months after his arrival in the neighborhood, it was understood by everyone that if Rex wasn't the leader of the gang, he was very nearly the leader. He had fought and licked every boy in the neighborhood who at one time or another had fancied himself leader. And he had done so without any noticeable ill-feeling, pride, or ambition.

As a matter of fact, no one could possibly have been more good-natured than Rex. Everybody resented him, just the same.

One winter, the whole neighborhood took to playing a game that had become popular on the other side of the tracks, in another slum neighborhood of the town: *Leapfrog.* The idea was for as many boys as cared to participate, to bend down and be leaped over by every other boy in the game, and then himself to get up and begin leaping over all the other boys, and then bend down again until all the boys had leaped over him again, and keep this up until all the other players had become exhausted. This didn't happen, sometimes, until the last two players had traveled a distance of three our four miles, while the other players walked along, watching and making bets.

Rosie, of course, was always in on the game. She was always one of the last to drop out, too. And she was the only person in the neighborhood Rex Folger hadn't fought and beaten.

He felt that that was much too humiliating even to think about. But inasmuch as she seemed to be a member of the gang, he felt that in some way or another he ought to prove his superiority.

One summer day during vacation, an argument between Rex and Rosie developed and Rosie pulled off her turtle-neck sweater and challenged him to a fight. Rex took a cigarette from his pocket, lighted it, inhaled, and told Rosie he wasn't in the habit of hitting women – where he came from that amounted to boxing your mother. On the other hand, he said, if Rosie cared to compete with him in any other sport, he would be glad to oblige her. Rex was a very calm and courteous conversationalist. He had poise. It was unconscious, of course, but he had it just the same. He was just naturally a man who couldn't be hurried, flustered, or excited.

So Rex and Rosie fought it out in this game Leapfrog. They got to leaping over one another, quickly, too, until the first thing we knew the whole gang of us was out on the State Highway going south towards Fowler. It was a very hot day. Rosie and Rex were in great shape, and it looked like one was tougher than the other and more stubborn. They talked a good deal, especially Rosie, who insisted that she would have to fall down unconscious before she'd give up to a guy like Rex.

He said he was sorry his opponent was a girl. It grieved him deeply to have to make a girl exert herself to the point of death, but it was just too bad. He had to, so he had to. They leaped and squatted, leaped and squatted, and we got out to Sam Day's vineyard. That was half-way to Fowler. It didn't seem like either Rosie or Rex was ever going to get tired. They hadn't even begun to show signs of growing tired, although each of them was sweating a great deal.

Naturally, we were sure Rex would win the contest. But that was because we hadn't taken into account the fact that he was a simple person, whereas Rosie was crafty and shrewd. Rosie knew how to figure angles. She had discovered how to jump over Rex Folger in a way that weakened him. And after a while, about three miles out of Fowler, we noticed that she was coming down on Rex's *neck,* instead of on his back. Naturally, this was hurting him and making the blood rush to his head. Rosie herself squatted in such a way that it was impossible, almost, for Rex to get anywhere near her neck with his hands.

Before long, we noticed that Rex was weakening. His head was getting closer and closer to the ground. About a half mile out of Fowler, we heard Rex's head bumping the ground every time Rosie leaped over him. They were good loud bumps that we knew were painful, but Rex wasn't complaining. He was too proud to complain.

Rosie, on the other hand, knew she had her man, and she was giving him all she had. She was bumping his head on the ground as solidly as she could, because she knew she didn't have much more fight in her, and if she didn't lay him out cold, in the hot sun, in the next ten minutes or so, she would fall down exhausted herself, and lose the contest.

Suddenly Rosie bumped Rex's head a real powerful one. He got up very dazed and very angry. It was the first time we had ever seen him fuming. By God, the girl was taking advantage of him, if he wasn't mistaken, and he didn't like it. Rosie was squatted in front of him. He came up groggy and paused a moment. Then he gave Rosie a very effective kick that sent her sprawling. Rosie jumped up and smacked Rex in the mouth. The gang jumped in and tried to establish order.

It was agreed that the Leapfrog contest must not change into a fight. Not any more. Not with Fowler only five or ten minutes away. The gang ruled further that Rex had had no right to kick Rosie and that in smacking him in the mouth Rosie had squared the matter, and the contest was to continue.

Rosie was very tired and sore; and so was Rex. They began leaping and squatting again; and again we saw Rosie coming down on Rex's neck so that his head was bumping the ground.

It looked pretty bad for the boy from Texas. We couldn't understand how he could take so much punishment. We all felt that Rex was getting what he had coming to him, but at the same time everybody seemed to feel badly about Rosie, a girl, doing the job instead of one of us. Of course, that was where we were wrong. Nobody but Rosie could have figured out that smart way of humiliating a very powerful and superior boy. It was probably the woman in her, which, less than five years later, came out to such an extent that she became one of the most beautiful girls in town, gave up tomboy activities, and married one of the wealthiest young men in Kings County, a college man named, if memory serves, Wallace Hadington Finlay VI.

Less than a hundred yards from the heart of Fowler, Rosie, with great and admirable artistry, finished the job.

That was where the dirt of the highway siding ended and the paved main street of Fowler began. This street was paved with cement, not asphalt. Asphalt, in that heat, would have been too soft to serve, but cement had exactly the right degree of brittleness. I think Rex, when he squatted over the hard cement, knew the game was up. But he was brave to the end. He squatted over the hard cement and waited for the worst. Behind him, Rosie Mahoney prepared to make the supreme effort. In this next leap, she intended to give her all, which she did.

She came down on Rex Folger's neck like a ton of bricks. His head banged against the hard cement, his body straightened out, and his arms and legs twitched.

He was out like a light.

Six paces in front of him, Rosie Mahoney squatted and waited. Jim Telesco counted twenty, which was the time allowed for each leap. Rex didn't get up during the count.

The contest was over. The winner of the contest was Rosie Mahoney.

Rex didn't get up by himself at all. He just stayed where he was until a half-dozen of us lifted him and carried him to a horse trough, where we splashed water on his face.

Rex was a confused young man all the way back. He was also a deeply humiliated one. He couldn't understand anything about anything. He just looked dazed and speechless. Every now and then we imagined he wanted to talk, and I guess he did, but after we'd all gotten ready to hear what he had to say, he couldn't speak. He made a gesture so tragic that tears came to the eyes of eleven members of the gang.

Rosie Mahoney, on the other hand, talked all the way home. She said everything.

I think it made a better man of Rex. More human. After that he was a gentler sort of soul. It may have been because he couldn't see very well for some time. At any rate, for weeks he seemed to be going around in a dream. His gaze would freeze on some insignificant object far away in the landscape, and half the time it seemed as if he didn't know where he was going, or why. He took little part in the activities of the gang, and the following winter he stayed away altogether. He came to school one day wearing glasses. He looked broken and pathetic.

That winter Rosie Mahoney stopped hanging around with the gang, too. She had a flair for making an exit at the right time.

Biographical Notes

William Saroyan (1908–1981) was born in California of Armenian parents. His father had come to America because of political persecution in his home country. At an early age he made up his mind to become a writer and started reading extensively. He had to leave school at 15 to earn his living, and worked at a number of jobs.

His literary career began when his collection of short stories The Daring Young Man on the Flying Trapeze *was published in 1934. In the years to follow, he published several more. His play* The Time of Your Life *won the highly-regarded Pulitzer Prize in 1939, but he refused it because he was opposed to patronage of the arts by business. His best-known work is* The Human Comedy *(1943), a novel which has been translated into many languages; it was later made into a film.*

Many of Saroyan's stories are semi-autobiographical, or deal with the kind of immigrant community he grew up in. In all of his works, he expresses something of his great love for the ordinary people of America.

Annotations

67 **leapfrog** children's game in which one player bends down and another jumps over him/her – **contest** ['––] competition – 1 **folks** *coll.* family; relatives or parents – 2 **innate** [ɪ'neɪt] part of one's nature – 4 **Southern Pacific** one of the major American railway companies – **G Street** In some American towns streets don't have proper names but are identified by numbers or letters. – 5 **turtle-neck sweater** ['swetə] pull-over with a high round collar – **bricklayer** person whose work is to build with bricks (Ziegelsteine) – 11 **clan** large family – 12 **for all that** in spite of this – 13 **studious, scholarly** fond of learning or studying – 15 **undesirable** not to be wished for – 16 **to make it a point to do s.th.** to make a special effort to do s.th. – 17 **daring** unusual, requiring courage – 18 **awkward** uncomfortable – 19 **to ask no quarter** not to expect pity – 21 **to whip** *here:* to beat, to defeat – **honest** *here:* fair – 22 **a draw** (of contests) undecided – **a slight edge** a little bit – 23 **opening** *here:* opportunity – 24 **to humiliate** [hjuː'mɪlɪeɪt] to make s.o. feel ashamed – 27 **to be in on s.th.** to take part in s.th. – **mischief** ['mɪstʃɪf] foolish behaviour, trouble, trickery – 30 **pitcher (in baseball)** player who throws the ball – **had a wicked wing** *coll.* was very good in wing (far-side) position – 32 **catcher's mitt** strong hand-covering worn by a baseball player

68 1 **swift** quick – 3 **pee-wee** game of marbles (Murmeln) – **disgusting** *here:* annoying – 6 **to embarrass** to make (s.o.) feel uncomfortable – 10 **to be the equal of** to be as good as – 19 **to lick** *coll.* to beat, to defeat – 20 **to fancy o.s.** to imagine oneself to be – 21

ambition strong desire for success – 23 **to resent** [rɪ'zent] to feel angry at or unhappy about – 24 **to take to** to take up, to start doing – 26 **to care to** to like, to want – 30 **exhausted** very tired – 38 **inasmuch as** since, because – 40 **argument** ['ɑ:gjʊmənt] quarrel

69 1 **to challenge s.o.** to call s.o. to take part in a fight or a contest – 4 **to amount to** to be the same as – 6 **to oblige** [ə'blaɪdʒ] to do s.o. a favour – **courteous** ['kɜ:tɪəs] polite – **conversationalist** one who is good at talking – 7 **poise** [pɔɪz] quiet self-confidence, ability to deal with all social situations – **unconscious** *here:* not done on purpose – 8 **to fluster s.o.** to make s.o. nervous – 13 **in great shape** in good form, physically fit – 14 **stubborn** strong-willed – 17 **to grieve** [i:] to make (s.o.) very unhappy – 18 **to exert o.s.** [–'–] to put all one's energy into s.th. – 19 **to squat** [ɒ] to bend down – 20 **vineyard** ['vɪnjəd] piece of land used for wine production – 25 **to take into account** to consider – 26 **crafty, shrewd** [ʃru:d] clever and tricky – **to figure angles** *here:* to leap at the angle most advantageous to herself – 38 **she had her man** *coll.* she had gained the upper hand – 39 **solid** firm, strong

70 1 **to lay s.o. out cold** *coll.* to knock s.o. unconscious – 4 **dazed** dizzy, unable to think clearly – **to fume** to be very angry – 8 **to sprawl** to lie with one's arms and legs stretched out – **to smack** to hit – 13 **to square the matter** to make things equal – 14 **sore** with aching muscles – 18 **punishment** *here:* ill treatment – 19 **he had [it] coming to him** *coll.* he deserved it – 21 **to figure out** *coll.* to work out – **smart** *coll.* clever – 23 **to such an extent that** so much that – 24 **tomboy** girl who is fond of rough and noisy games – 28 **admirable** ['– – – –] excellent – 29 **siding** soft sand or earth along the side of a road – 32 **brittleness** hardness – 33 **the game was up** *coll.* the game was lost – 39 **to twitch** to make small, uncontrolled movements

71 1 **pace** step – 6 **trough** [trɒf] open box for animals to drink from – 18 **at any rate** in any case – 19 **gaze** long steady look – **insignificant** not important – 23 **pathetic** [pə'θetɪk] sad, pitiful – 25 **flair** instinct for effective behaviour

Interpretation and Teaching Notes

Summary and Analysis

A familiar children's rhyme expresses the conventional belief of what boys and girls should be like:

Sugar and spice and all things nice,
that's what little girls are made of.
Frogs and snails and puppy-dogs' tails,
that's what little boys are made of.

Saroyan's "The Great Leapfrog Contest" is an affectionate, humorous, and sentimental story of a young girl, Rosie Mahoney, who is more "frogs and snails" than "sugar and spice and all things nice." She is a "tough little Irish [-American] kid" growing up in the ethnically mixed community we can assume is Fresno, California (Saroyan's home town) in the first quarter of the century. Rosie is a tomboy, i.e. a young, generally pre-adolescent girl who sees no reason she can't do the same things that boys do. Or, as the story relates, beat the best of them at their own game.

Rosie is the youngest child of a working-class family living in the poorer part of town (i.e. 'on the other side of the tracks'). The family "secmed to be a happy one", and is portrayed in near caricature as large (three grown brothers and two married sisters in addition to Rosie), with a father who drinks, and a religious mother named Mary. Rosie lives in a neighbourhood that is still pre-urban, pre-surfing, California. The children of upward-moving immigrant families make do-it-yourself fun with whatever is at hand, be it a tin-can instead of a hockey stick, or a contest between the two toughest kids at, for example, leapfrog.

Rosie has already proved to the boys in her "gang" that she is as good as they are, if not better, at various popular sports and games, and in the everyday 'horse-play' of pre-adolescent boys. Then the new boy in the neighbourhood, Rex Folger, appears to challenge her position. Rex (the king?) only needs to beat Rosie to be the undisputed top kid in the neighbourhood, but with his courtly Southern-gentleman manners, he does not want to fight a girl. (This being a more formalized version of the male-chauvinist attitudes barely overcome — or suppressed – by the other boys: **67** 17–18, 23–24; **68** 6–8; **70** 19–20.) Nevertheless, the conflict must come, and it comes when the two agree to have it out in a leapfrog contest. With the gang in attendance, Rosie, "crafty and shrewd", outwits "simple" Rex by rather unsportingly coming down on his neck. His male pride plays into her hands (**68** 17–19, 37). Finally, after much such punishment, the boy from Texas is finished off. "She came down on Rex Folger's neck like a ton of bricks." He was "out like a light", and Rosie was the winner. She had beaten the best of them, at his own game, in her own way. And in spite of themselves, they admired her for it. The immediate and long term effects of this defeat on Rex seem to have been devastating, but this does not seem to matter much to anybody. As for Rosie, there is a suggestion that she went on to find even better ways of manipulating the system to her own ends (**68** 20–26).

In interpreting this story, restraint must be used. One should not look for a clear-cut message on sex-role prejudice or violence among children, even if these are major elements in the humour. Rather, Rosie is obviously a favourite 'character' among the author's/narrator's childhood memories, who won the boys' respect despite the late-Victorian social conventions to which they were all heirs, and partly with the help of these conventions, which she cleverly turns to her own advantage.

One should note that in the U.S., and especially in the West, to be a tomboy was certainly not frowned upon to the degree that it was — and often still is — in other societies and cultures. Rosie is much more the plucky underdog, the high-spirited, clever, never-say-die individual who outwits an opponent at great odds. The character is a favourite one in America, and again, especially so in the trans-Mississippi West. Here many 19th-century humorists found their heroes among the common people, and burlesqued those who, imagining themselves to be superior, were easily outwitted. Saroyan was certainly familiar with Mark Twain's work, and it is interesting to note that "The Notorious Jumping Frog of Calaveras County" (1865) was set only some 170 km. north-west of Fresno. There are certainly parallels in the content: the "frog" element, the seemingly sure defeat of the underdog (or under-frog), and the final outwitting of the once-sure winner, a 'slick talker' , who is left confused and humiliated. Above all, they share the lightly ironic humour, the artistry of the afterthought and wry comment, a mark of the American, oral-humour tradition:

> I think it made a better man of Rex. More human. After that he was a gentler sort of soul. It may have been because he couldn't see very well for some time. (**71** 16–18)

Tongue-in-cheek exaggeration — tall tales not expected to be taken seriously by anyone except a greenhorn outsider — are also part of this tradition. Fowler is approximately 15 km. south of Fresno on what is today State Highway 99. Maybe Rex and Rosie (or some kids just like them) *did* leapfrog that distance on a very hot summer's day. Or, perhaps it just makes a better story like that. The story is light humour, a tale very well-told by someone looking back in fondness at the friends of his youth, while poking a bit of fun at the boys they were, their unconscious attitudes, their secret resentments and maliciousness. He does not exclude himself from the fun — witness the nonchalant callousness of his closing remarks (**71** 8–23), which are obviously meant to cause raised eyebrows at the very least. With a last deft touch of humour, he and Rosie make their exit at the same right time.

Unit I
Rosie and the Boys (Exposition)

Preparation: Students should have read to **68** 14.

1. Reader's expectations
What does the title of the story lead the reader to expect?
There is something funny about connecting "great" and "leapfrog contest" together, since leapfrog is a young children's game and not a serious sport. It might therefore be a humorous story about children, using intentional exaggeration as a humorous device.

2. Rosie Mahoney
What do we learn about Rosie in the first page and a half?
There is very little physical description of Rosie. "Tough little kid" (**67** 1), together with the behaviour described, suggests she was aged 11—14 (pre- or early teens). We learn a lot about her family background which may include possible explanations for her being a tomboy (as the youngest child of elderly parents, her companionship and 'models' were probably outside the home to a larger degree than with most children; or maybe the happy-go-lucky atmosphere of her working-class family was just not conducive to feminine gentility.) Her prowess in all types of sports is given great emphasis. We learn that she is plucky, that is, always willing to accept a dare, put up a good fight, take a chance, etc. It is also stressed that Rosie is stubborn, single-minded and not easily defeated (**67** 16–20, 26; **68** 5–6; 12–14). Being of Irish descent probably helps – according to the cliché of the hot-tempered, 'fighting Irish'.

3. The gang

What other main characters are introduced at the beginning? What do you learn about them?

Only Rosie's parents are named, but they play no further role in the story. The emphasis is on Rosie's relationship with a gang of boys. The narrator is obviously one of them: he refers to them either as "the boys" (**67** 16), "everybody" (**67** 17), or "we" (**68** 4). We learn that they all felt rather uneasy about a girl taking part in their games (**67** 17–19): their vague notions of male pride and honour (and female vulnerability) made them feel equally bad about treating her roughly (**68** 6–8) and being treated roughly by her (**67** 23–24). But gradually they come to accept her as a member of the gang. Note that the boys' unconscious sexism, which made it difficult for Rosie at first, was very soon turned to Rosie's advantage (**67** 24–25). This is relevant for the further development of the story.

4. Function of details

In what ways does the author make the reader believe that his characters are 'real people'?

The story is told by a narrator who claims to remember all of this from his childhood days and to have been directly involved himself (e. g. "my home town", "... the game we invented and used to call ..."). 'True' stories are also marked by seemingly irrelevant information (e. g. the parents' names; the father's profession; the turtle-neck sweater). This gives the impression that the narrator is relating anything he happens to remember. All that is required is that these details be plausible. Who would doubt, for example, that there was a "G Street", or a "Greek Orthodox Catholic Church on Kearny Boulevard", especially if you know that "G streets" are so common, and that many California streets are named after Stephen Kearny, a famous general in the Mexican-American War? In short, Saroyan's narrator is using a standard tale-teller's technique; if the audience gets enough specific details, especially ones that are not central to the story, they will not tend to question the larger elements.

5. Free discussion

How do you feel about Rosie at this point in the story?
Do you like her? Dislike her? Do you know someone/remember someone like her? What do you think of the boys' attitude?
Are young boys still as wary of girls as in this story? Why?

Homework: Read the story to the end.

Unit II
Rosie and Rex (Action and Denouement)

1. The structure of the story

How does the rest of the story differ from the part discussed in the last lesson?

The first section just presents the necessary background, and could be called the 'exposition'; **68** 15 is where the action starts — the "contest" itself.

2. Rex Folger

Describe 'the new boy in town'.

Rex is an outsider who very rapidly establishes himself, by fighting and by force of personality, as "very near" the leader of the gang, with Rosie the only remaining challenger. Though he did not show "noticeable ill-feeling, pride, or ambition" and was extremely good-natured, the boys still resented him. (Someone who wins most of the time and has no obvious faults will of course be easily disliked by people who don't always win and are less than perfect.)

Rex can't bring himself, as all the other boys have (however unwillingly), to fight Rosie. He "felt that that was much too humiliating even to think about", and is only willing to compete against Rosie as long as it doesn't involve a fist fight (**68** 37–39). The 'male chauvinist' instincts common to all of the boys seem in Rex's case to have been crystallized into a rigid code of honour.

Considering where Rex came from, and his reputed style of speaking, as well as the overt indicator, "where he came from that amounted to boxing your mother" (**69** 3–4), it can be argued that Rex is under the influence of the traditional Southern code of chivalry — an American offshoot of the Cavalier tradition. To hit a lady is to be a cad, a weakling, and unworthy of the company of gentlemen. Rosie thus has Rex in a quandary, for nothing in the code says how one acts when a lady attacks a gentleman. If he were to fight and win, he would lose (he believes) the respect of his fellows. And to lose to a woman would be unbearable. It can be added that women familiar with this code of behaviour find it rather easy to make its adherents look rather foolish.

3. The contest and its outcome

How does Rosie manage to win the contest that the boys were sure she would lose?

Rosie outwits her opponent by playing the game in a rather unsporting manner, coming down on his neck instead of his back as she was supposed to (**69** 26). Furthermore, she knew his weakness as a male: "He was too proud to complain" (**69** 37) that a girl was physically hurting him. When he does finally realize that he is being taken advantage of (**70** 3–8), he drops his code of honour for a moment. Ironically, and comically, the gang points out that he had no right to hit Rosie. In other words, they remind him of his own sexist rules which Rosie was taking advantage of. When Rosie finally puts him away, "brave to the end", it is almost as if he were a punch-drunk boxer: "Rex didn't get up during the count" (**70** 33–**71** 3). [If desired, the outcome of the contest can be referred to as the 'denouement' of the story.]

4. Discussion: revision of first impressions
After Rosie has won the contest, how do you feel about her?
Has your initial impression changed? If so, why?
[It might be expected — or even hoped – that there is some divergence of opinion at this point among male and female students. The males might have some (disguised?) sympathy for a "very powerful and superior boy" (**70** 22) who has been humiliated in such an underhanded way. Girls are more likely to feel that Rex had it coming to him, and to feel especially gratified that Rosie was able to turn his overbearing vanity to her own advantage. On the other hand, some female students might even resent Rosie for having to some extent employed traditional female tactics (manipulating male weaknesses). The fact that Rex was knocked out by having his head smashed against concrete should certainly gain him some sympathy, regardless of the principles involved, and make Rosie and her sympathizers seem a bit heartless.]

Homework: Go through the story and pick out those places where we get to hear the thoughts, feelings and opinions of
a) the narrator (exclude his account of events)
b) "the gang"
c) Rex
d) Rosie
[Allocate a), b), c), d) to different students. A certain overlapping is inevitable, and will be dealt with in the course of the following unit.]

Unit III
The Narrator

1. Narrator and author

Who is telling the story?

What is his own role in it?

The narrator is a man reminiscing about his childhood, when he was one of a gang of boys in some unnamed but recognizably Californian town (**67** 4: “Southern Pacific”; **69** 20: “Sam Day’s vineyard”). In the story, he closely identifies with this gang, referring to them as “we”, “we all”, “everybody” (e.g. **70** 17, 18, 19, 20) as well as “the boys” (**67** 16) and “the gang” (**68** 38). Like most of the others, the narrator’s position with regard to the main events of the story, the “contest”, is one of onlooker and, at most, umpire (cf. **70** 8–13).

How can you tell he is now an adult?

From the start, the use of the past tense (**67** 1: “Rosie Mahoney was ...”) indicates that all of this is over and done with. Near the end of the story it becomes clear that it is being told a lot more than five years later (**70** 22–26). Apart from that, a lot of the language, whether descriptive or explanatory, betrays the adult viewpoint (e.g. **67** 2; **68** 20–21; 22–23, 27–28; **71** 16–17, 19–20).

Could it be the author speaking?

One is certainly given this impression. [One could point out that the author’s home town was Fresno, California, that the Southern Pacific railroad goes through this city, and that there is a small town named Fowler nearby — and then ask how it affects their enjoyment of the story to know that it may very well have happened. One should then point out that many authors *deliberately* give rise to such an impression in order to increase the plausibility of their *fiction*.]

2. Narrative technique

Which characters actually speak in this story? Is there, in fact, any direct dialogue?

The only character who actually speaks in the story is the narrator. He only speaks to the reader, and never to the characters directly. Whether he expresses his own ideas or those of others, we know both only from what he tells us. There are a few instances where he appears to be reporting the characters’ actual words (Rex: **69** 34, 17–19; Rosie: **69** 15–16). Otherwise he tells us what he thinks they thought and felt (e.g. **67** 14–15, 26–27; **68** 37–39). It is understandable that he tells us most about what the other boys were thinking, since he identifies so closely with them (e.g. **67** 24–25; **68** 6–8, 17–19, 23).

3. Effect of narrative technique

What effect does it have on the reader to see the entire story through the narrator's eyes?

Our information on what happens, and what happened, is dependent upon his view as a child *and* as an adult. As the story progresses, and especially during the leapfrog contest, we tend to forget for a moment that we are seeing it through the narrator's memory, and so we experience these events as if we were there with him. When the narrator periodically returns to his initial, retrospective point of view, clearly commenting on the characters (e.g. **70** 22–26) rather than 'reporting', many readers will suddenly feel more free to disagree with his views (e.g. **70** 22–23: "It was probably the woman in her ...") and may become more critical of his rather callous attitude to Rex after his downfall — or amused by it.

[At this point one should make an attempt — with the aid of the students' homework — to separate the opinions of the narrator himself from the communal view of the gang. In many cases it will be found that this is impossible.

For example, "It was agreed that ..." (**70** 10) could either be 'filled' by "by us" (the boys including narrator) or "by them" (the boys from the narrator's view) or "by the gang" (either one). Similar difficulties apply to the attempt to discern the narrator's 'adult' voice from those passages where he is reliving the emotions of his youth. Given such normal difficulties, it is suggested that students be merely asked for a few examples of each, and not be expected to carry out a full analysis. In order to develop their awareness of such differences, and the effect of switching from one to the other, it might be useful to have one short selection from the story in which all three views are clearly at work. One such selection (**71** 9–13):

> He couldn't understand anything about anything. He just looked dazed and speechless. Every now and then we imagined he wanted to talk, and I guess he did, but after we'd all gotten ready to hear what he had to say he couldn't speak. He made a gesture so tragic that tears came to the eyes of eleven members of the gang.

The irony in the last sentence clearly suggests the viewpoint of the adult looking back, and smiling at the memory.]

4. Free discussion

Which of the narrator's opinions do you agree with or disagree with?

If some prompting is necessary, "It was probably the woman in her ..." (**70** 22ff.) should certainly attract some outraged comments, as it implies that sly manipulation of the weaknesses of one's opponent (or one's prey — in the case of Wallace Hadington Finlay VI!) is something typically female. It could then be discussed whether such tactics are (or were) often adopted by women as a means of survival in a society which is (or was) basically hostile to their interests.

67 17–19, 24; **68** 6–8: The narrator seems to assume that it is particularly "humiliating" for a boy to be beaten by a girl. Why should this be so?

71 16–23: Considering that Rex seems to have suffered something like serious brain damage, isn't the narrator being a bit callous here? Or is this meant ironically?

Which character do you think the author likes better, Rosie or Rex?

Which one do you *like better? Why?*

What do you think of the narrator himself as a character?

Additional Homework (Grammar Revision):

What the various characters said is given in reported speech only. Find examples of this (cf. Unit III, point 2) and reconstruct the actual words spoken (direct speech).

Katherine Mansfield

Her First Ball

Exactly when the ball began Leila would have found it hard to say. Perhaps her first real partner was the cab. It did not matter that she shared the cab with the Sheridan girls and their brother. She sat back in her own little corner of it, and the bolster on which her hand rested felt like the sleeve of an unknown young man's dress suit; and away they bowled, past waltzing lamp-posts and houses and fences and trees.

"Have you really never been to a ball before, Leila? But, my child, how too weird –" cried the Sheridan girls.

"Our nearest neighbour was fifteen miles," said Leila softly, gently opening and shutting her fan.

Oh dear, how hard it was to be indifferent like the others! She tried not to smile too much; she tried not to care. But every single thing was so new and exciting. Meg's tuberoses, Jose's long loop of amber, Laura's little dark head, pushing above her white fur like a flower through snow. She would remember for ever. It even gave her a pang to see her cousin Laurie throw away the wisps of tissue paper he pulled from the fastenings of his new gloves. She would like to have kept those wisps as a keepsake, as a remembrance. Laurie leaned forward and put his hand on Laura's knee.

"Look here, darling," he said. "The third and the ninth as usual. Twig?"

Oh, how marvellous to have a brother! In her excitement Leila felt that if there had been time, if it hadn't been impossible, she couldn't have helped crying because she was an only child and no brother had ever said "Twig?" to her; no sister would ever say, as Meg said to Jose that moment, "I've never known your hair go up more successfully than it has tonight."

But, of course, there was no time. They were at the drill hall already; there were cabs in front of them and cabs behind. The road was bright on either side with moving fanlike lights, and on the pavement gay couples seemed to float through the air; little satin shoes chased each other like birds.

"Hold on to me, Leila; you'll get lost," said Laura.

"Come on, girls, let's make a dash for it," said Laurie.

Leila put two fingers on Laura's pink velvet cloak, and they were somehow lifted past the big golden lantern, carried along the passage, and pushed into the little room marked 'Ladies'. Here the crowd was so great there was hardly space to take off their things; the noise was deafening. Two benches on either side were stacked high with wraps. Two old women in white aprons ran up and down tossing fresh armfuls. And everybody was pressing forward trying to get at the little dressing-table and mirror at the far end.

A great quivering jet of gas lighted the ladies' room. It couldn't wait; it was dancing already. When the door opened again and there came a burst of tuning from the drill hall, it leaped almost to the ceiling.

Dark girls, fair girls were patting their hair, tying ribbons again, tucking handkerchiefs down the fronts of their bodices, smoothing marble-white gloves. And because they were all laughing it seemed to Leila that they were all lovely.

"Aren't there any invisible hairpins?" cried a voice. "How most extraordinary! I can't see a single invisible hairpin."

"Powder my back, there's a darling," cried someone else.

"But I must have a needle and cotton. I've torn simply miles and miles of the frill," wailed a third.

Then, "Pass them along, pass them along!" The straw basket of programmes was tossed from arm to arm. Darling little pink-and-silver programmes, with pink pencils and fluffy tassels. Leila's fingers shook as she took one out of the basket. She wanted to ask someone, "Am I meant to have one too?" but she had just time to read: 'Waltz 3. *Two, Two in a Canoe*. Polka 4. *Making the Feathers Fly,'* when Meg cried, "Ready, Leila?" and they pressed their way through the crush in the passage towards the big double doors of the drill hall.

Dancing had not begun yet, but the band had stopped tuning, and the noise was so great it seemed that when it did begin to play it would never be heard. Leila, pressing close to Meg, looking over Meg's shoulder, felt that even the little quivering coloured flags strung across the ceiling were talking. She quite forgot to be shy; she forgot how in the middle of dressing she had sat down on the bed with one shoe off and one shoe on and begged her mother to ring up her cousins and say she couldn't go after all. And the rush of longing she had had to be sitting on the veranda of their forsaken up-country home, listening to the baby owls crying 'More pork' in the moonlight, was changed to a rush of joy so sweet that it was hard to bear alone. She clutched her fan, and, gazing at the gleaming, golden floor, the azaleas, the lanterns, the stage at one end with its red carpet and gilt chairs and the band in a corner, she thought breathlessly, 'How heavenly; how simply heavenly!'

All the girls stood grouped together at one side of the doors, the men at the other, and the chaperones in dark dresses, smiling rather foolishly, walked with little careful steps over the polished floor towards the stage.

"This is my little country cousin Leila. Be nice to her. Find her partners; she's under my wing," said Meg going up to one girl after another.

Strange faces smiled at Leila – sweetly, vaguely. Strange voices answered, "Of course, my dear." But Leila felt the girls didn't really see her. They were looking towards the men. Why didn't the men begin? What were they waiting for? There they stood, smoothing their gloves, patting their glossy hair and smiling among themselves. Then, quite suddenly, as if they had only just made up their minds that that was what they had to do, the men came gliding over the parquet. There was a joyful flutter among the girls. A tall, fair man flew up to Meg, seized her programme, scribbled something; Meg passed him on to Leila. "May I have the pleasure?" He ducked and smiled. There came a dark man wearing an eyeglass, then cousin Laurie came with a friend, and Laura with a little freckled fellow whose tie was crooked. Then quite an old man – fat, with a big bald patch on his head – took her programme and murmured, "Let me see, let me see!" And he was a long time comparing his programme, which looked black with names, with hers. It seemed to give him so much trouble that Leila was ashamed. "Oh, please don't bother," she said eagerly. But instead of replying the fat man wrote something, glanced at her again. "Do I remember this bright little face?" he said softly. " Is it known to me of yore?" At that moment the band began playing; the fat man disappeared. He was tossed away on a great wave of music that came flying over the gleaming floor, breaking the groups up into couples, scattering them, sending them spinning. . . .

Leila had learned to dance at boarding school. Every Saturday afternoon the boarders were hurried off to a little corrugated iron mission hall where Miss Eccles (of London) held her 'select' classes. But the difference between that dusty-smelling hall – with calico texts on the walls, the poor, terrified little woman in a brown velvet toque with rabbit's ears, thumping the cold piano, Miss Eccles poking the girls' feet with her long white wand – and this, was so tremendous that Leila was sure if her partner didn't come and she had to listen to that marvellous music and to watch the others sliding, gliding over the golden floor, she would die at least, or faint, or lift her arms and fly out of one of those dark windows that showed the stars.

"Ours, I think –" Someone bowed, smiled, and offered her his arm; she hadn't to die after all. Someone's hand pressed her waist, and she floated away like a flower that is tossed into a pool.

"Quite a good floor, isn't it?" drawled a faint voice close to her ear.

"I think it's most beautifully slippery," said Leila.

"Pardon!" The faint voice sounded surprised. Leila said it again. And there was a tiny pause before the voice echoed, "Oh, quite!" and she was swung round again.

He steered so beautifully. There was the great difference between dancing with girls and men, Leila decided. Girls banged into each other and stamped on each other's feet; the girl who was the gentleman always clutched you so.

The azaleas were separate flowers no longer; they were pink and white flags streaming by.

"Were you at the Bells' last week?" the voice came again. It sounded tired. Leila wondered whether she ought to ask him if he would like to stop.

"No, this is my first dance," said she.

Her partner gave a little gasping laugh. "Oh, I say," he protested.

"Yes, it is really the first dance I've ever been to." Leila was most fervent. It was such a relief to be able to tell somebody. "You see, I've lived in the country all my life up till now . . ."

At that moment the music stopped and they went to sit on two chairs against the wall. Leila tucked her pink satin feet under and fanned herself, while she blissfully watched the other couples passing and disappearing through the swing doors.

"Enjoying yourself, Leila?" asked Jose, nodding her golden head.

Laura passed and gave her the faintest little wink; it made Leila wonder for a moment whether she was quite grown up after all. Certainly her partner did not say very much. He coughed, tucked his handkerchief away, pulled down his waistcoat, took a minute thread off his sleeve. But it didn't matter. Almost immediately the band started and her second partner seemed to spring from the ceiling.

"Floor's not bad," said the new voice. Did one always begin with the floor? And then, "Were you at the Neaves' on Tuesday?" And again Leila explained. Perhaps it was a little strange that her partners were not more interested. For it was thrilling. Her first ball! She was only at the beginning of everything. It seemed to her that she had never known what the night was like before. Up till now it had been dark, silent, beautiful very often – oh yes – but mournful somehow. Solemn. And now it would never be like that again – it had opened dazzling bright.

"Care for an ice?" said her partner. And they went through the swing doors, down the passage, to the supper-room. Her cheeks burned, she was fearfully thirsty. How sweet the ices looked on little glass plates and how cold the frosted spoon was, iced too! And when they came back to the hall there was the fat man waiting for her by the door. It gave her quite a shock again to see how old he was; he ought to have been on the stage with the fathers and mothers. And when Leila compared him with her other partners he looked shabby. His waistcoat was creased, there was a button off his glove, his coat looked as if it was dusty with French chalk.

"Come along, little lady," said the fat man. He scarcely troubled to clasp her, and they moved away so gently, it was more like walking than dancing. But he said not a word about the floor. "Your first dance, isn't it?" he murmured.

"How *did* you know?"

"Ah," said the fat man, "that's what it is to be old!" He wheezed faintly as he steered her past an awkward couple. "You see, I've been doing this kind of thing for the last thirty years."

"Thirty years?" cried Leila. Twelve years before she was born!

"It hardly bears thinking about, does it?" said the fat man gloomily. Leila looked at his bald head, and she felt quite sorry for him.

"I think it's marvellous to be still going on," she said kindly.

"Kind little lady," said the fat man, and he pressed her a little closer and hummed a bar of the waltz. "Of course," he said, "you can't hope to last anything like as long as that. No-o," said the fat man, "long before that you'll be sitting up there on the stage, looking on, in your nice black velvet. And these pretty arms will have turned into little short fat ones, and you'll beat time with such a different kind of fan – a black ebony one." The fat man seemed to shudder. "And you'll smile away like the poor old dears up there, and point to your daughter, and tell the elderly lady next to you how some dreadful man tried to kiss her at the club ball. And your heart will ache, ache" – the fat man squeezed her closer still, as if he really was sorry for that poor heart – "because no one wants to kiss you now. And you'll say how unpleasant these polished floors are to walk on, how dangerous they are. Eh, Mademoiselle Twinkletoes?" said the fat man softly.

Leila gave a light little laugh, but she did not feel like laughing. Was it – could it all be true? It sounded terribly true. Was this first ball only the beginning of her last ball, after all? At that the music seemed to change; it sounded sad, sad; it rose upon a great sigh. Oh, how quickly things changed! Why didn't happiness last for ever? For ever wasn't a bit too long.

"I want to stop," she said in a breathless voice. The fat man led her to the door.

"No," she said, "I won't go outside. I won't sit down. I'll just stand here, thank you." She leaned against the wall, tapping with her foot, pulling up her gloves and trying to smile. But deep inside her a little girl threw her pinafore over her head and sobbed. Why had he spoiled it all?

"I say, you know," said the fat man, "you mustn't take me seriously, little lady."

"As if I should!" said Leila, tossing her small dark head and sucking her underlip. . . .

Again the couples paraded. The swing doors opened and shut. Now new music was given out by the bandmaster. But Leila didn't want to dance any more. She wanted to be home, or sitting on the veranda listening to those baby owls. When she looked through the dark windows at the stars they had long beams like wings . . .

But presently a soft, melting, ravishing tune began, and a young man with curly hair bowed before her. She would have to dance, out of politeness, until she could find Meg. Very stiffly she walked into the middle; very haughtily she put her hand on his sleeve. But in one minute, in one turn, her feet glided, glided. The lights, the azaleas, the dresses, the pink faces, the velvet chairs, all became one beautiful flying wheel. And when her next partner bumped her into the fat man and he said, "Par*don*", she smiled at him more radiantly than ever. She didn't even recognize him again.

Biographical Notes

Katherine Mansfield (1888–1923) is New Zealand's most famous writer. She was the third daughter of a wealthy banker. Her talent first showed at the age of nine, when she won a prize for a school composition.

At the age of fifteen she was sent to school in London. Here she contributed stories to the college literary magazine. At the same time she trained as a cellist at the Royal Academy of Music.

After a two years' stay in New Zealand, she returned to London in 1908. She toured with an opera company and accepted unimportant roles in films to augment her father's annual grant of £100. This period was marked by the death of her beloved brother Leslie in World War I and a number of unhappy love affairs. In 1918 she married the critic, John Middleton Murry. Together with another well-known writer, D. H. Lawrence, they founded a literary magazine.

Her first published book was In a German Pension *(1911), a selection of travel impressions. Her best stories are to be found in the collections* Bliss and Other Stories *(1920),* The Garden Party and Other Stories *(1922),* The Dove's Nest and Other Stories *(1923), and* Something Childish and Other Stories *(published in 1924 after her death).*

From the point of view of literary history, Katherine Mansfield's stories mark a movement away from longer plot-oriented stories to a more psychological description of what has been called a "moment of felt life" (Henry James). She developed new techniques to show the more intimate feelings of her characters.

She died at the age of thirty-five in Fontainebleau, France, where she had gone for medical treatment after suffering from tuberculosis for several years.

Annotations

74 2 **cab** horse-drawn carriage for hire (*modern meaning:* taxi) – 4 **bolster** ['bəʊlstə] kind of cushion – 5 **dress suit** man's formal evening clothes – **to bowl** to move quickly on wheels – 8 **weird** [wɪəd] strange – 10 **fan** instrument used to cool one's face by making the air move – 11 **indifferent** showing no interest or emotion – 13 **Meg** from 'Margaret' – **tuberose** white, sweet-smelling flower (Nachthyazinthe) – **Jose** from 'Josephine' – **loop** *here:* necklace – **amber** yellowish-brown glassy substance used for jewels (Bernstein) – 14 **fur** [fɜ:] jacket or stole made of fur (Pelz) – 15 **pang** sudden feeling of pain – **Laurie** ['lɔ:rɪ] boy's name, short for 'Laurence' – 16 **wisp** small untidy piece of – **tissue paper** thin soft paper used for packing things – 17 **keepsake** souvenir – 19 **Twig?** *sl.* Understand? – 25 **drill hall** gymnasium (Turnhalle) – 27 **gay** happy, cheerful – 31 **to make a dash** to rush, to run quickly – **32 velvet** soft, thick cloth usually made of silk (Samt) – **cloak** loose, sleeveless outer garment (Umhang)

75 2 **to deafen** ['defən] to make deaf, i.e. unable to hear – 3 **to stack** to pile up – **wrap** outer garment, cloak – 4 **apron** ['eɪprən] s.th. worn over one's clothes to keep them clean – **to toss** to throw carelessly – 7 **to quiver** to tremble a little – **jet** *here:* narrow stream (of gas) – 9 **tuning** *here:* the sound of musicians preparing their instruments before a performance (**to tune** = stimmen) – 10 **to pat** to touch carefully with the flat of one's hand – **to tuck** to put s.th. where il will be held tightly – 11 **bodice** ['bɒdɪs] close-fitting upper part of a dress – **to smooth** [smu:ð] to straighten out – 16 **there's a darling** *here:* would you be so nice? – 18 **frill** ornamental edge to a dress (Rüsche) – **to wail** *here:* to say in a complaining voice – 20 **darling** *here: coll.* lovely, sweet – 21 **fluffy** soft and feathery – **tassel** little ornament made of threads fastened together – 25 **crush** *here:* lots of people crowding into a small space – 34 **forsaken** [fɔ:'seɪkən] lonely – 35 **owl** [aʊl] night bird with large eyes – 37 **to clutch** to hold tightly – **to gleam** to shine – 38 **gilt** with gold paint

76 2 **chaperone** ['ʃæpərəʊn] older woman who looks after a young unmarried woman in public – 9 **glossy** smooth and shiny – 12 **parquet** ['pɑ:keɪ] *here:* the dance floor – **flutter** nervous excitement – 13 **fair** fair-haired, blond – **to seize** [i:] to take hold of, to grab – 14 **to duck** to lower one's head quickly – 16 **freckled** with small brown marks on the skin – 17 **crooked** ['krʊkɪd] not straight – **bald patch** hairless spot on the scalp – 21 **to bother** *here:* to trouble o.s. – 23 **of yore** *arch., poet.* from the past, long ago – 26 **to scatter** to send in all directions – **to spin** to turn round and round fast – 29 **corrugated iron** Wellblech – 29 **select** exclusive – 30 **calico text** ['kælɪkəʊ] mottos or slogans embroidered on calico (a heavy cotton cloth) – 31 **toque** [təʊk] small, close-fitting hat – **to thump** to strike heavily – 32 **to poke** to push sharply – **wand** [ɒ] thin stick – 33 **tremendous** [–'– –] great – 37 **to bow** [baʊ] to bend forward as a sign of respect – 40 **to drawl** [drɔ:l] to speak slowly, dragging out the vowels – **faint** weak, not clear

77 15 **fervent** ['fɜ:vənt] earnest, with genuine feeling – 20 **blissful** very happy – 23 **wink** sign made by closing one eye briefly – 26 **waistcoat** Weste – **minute** [maɪ'nju:t] very small – **thread** [θred] (Faden) – 32 **thrilling** very exciting – 35 **mournful** sad, sorrowful – **solemn** ['sɒləm] serious, very impressive – 36 **dazzling** hurting one's eyes with strong light – 37 **(Would you) Care for ...?** Would you like ...?

78 4 **creased** [kri:st] full of lines made by folding – 5 **French chalk** chalk used by tailors for marking lines on cloth – 6 **to clasp** to hold firmly – 11 **to wheeze** breathe noisily – 12 **awkward** unskilful, inelegant – 15 **It hardly bears thinking about** It is not very pleasant to think about. – **gloomy** sad, melancholy – 19 **a bar** a few notes of music (Takt) – 23 **to beat time** to mark the musical rhythm – **ebony** ['ebənɪ] a hard heavy wood – 24 **to shudder** to shake as from horror – 26 **dreadful** awful, unpleasant – 27 **to ache** [eɪk] *here:* to be sad – 34 **sigh** Seufzer

79 1 **pinafore** ['pɪnəfɔ:] a child's apron – **to sob** to weep with short breaths – 10 **beam** ray, stream of light – 11 **presently** soon – **ravishing** [æ] very beautiful – 14 **haughty** ['hɔ:tɪ] acting in a superior fashion – 18 **radiant** showing great happiness

Interpretation and Teaching Notes

Summary and Analysis

A carriage is taking Leila, an eighteen-year-old country-girl (**78** 14) to her first ball in town. A little enviously the girl notes the elegant clothes and the self-assurance of her older cousins who are accompanying her. Arriving at the hall, Leila is stunned by the noise and crush in the ladies' room which mixes with the sound of instruments being tuned in the hall. Excitedly Leila chooses a programme from a straw basket before she and her cousin Meg press their way to the dance floor. In amazement the shy young girl takes in the splendour of the hall with its "gleaming golden floor" (**75** 37), the red carpet of the stage, the gilt chairs, the orchestra, the separate groups of men and girls, and the chaperones. A moment later, the men come over the parquet to the hopeful-looking girls and begin to write the names of their selected partners into their programmes. Finally, an old, almost bald-headed fat man accosts Leila and carefully checks his programme before entering her name.

When the ball begins, Leila revels in the huge difference from the "dusty-smelling hall" (**76** 30) where she had had dancing lessons at boarding school. A little later, she too is among the dancing couples and, though slightly puzzled by the stock phrases of her partners, she blissfully experiences "her first ball", "the beginning of everything" (**77** 32). But then the appearance of the old man in his shabby clothes wrenches her from her ecstasy. Though first pleased that somebody is taking her seriously, she is shocked by the obvious truth of what he prophesies during their dance: that the time will soon come when she will be a middle-aged lady watching the ball from the stage, hiding her sadness behind idle gossip and derogatory remarks about the floor. Dismayed by the thought that this is really "the beginning of her last ball" (**70** 32–33), Leila stops dancing. A feeling of sadness and homesickness seizes her. When finally "a soft, melting ravishing tune" (**79** 11) sets in and a young man appears before her, it is at first merely out of politeness that she accepts his invitation to dance. But then all becomes "one beautiful flying wheel" (**79** 16), so that she does not even recognize the old man when she bumps into him later.

The rigidly conventional turn-of-century world which is the setting of this story must appear to young readers like a fossil. But it is just this fossil-like character which should help to make clear the essentially artificial and arbitrary nature of all social conventions – even those we hardly notice, or take for granted today. At the same time, we see how they help to make the world go round, as it were. For Leila, the conventions of the ball are a step on the road towards adulthood, their mastery or assimilation a kind of initiation ceremony.

Within the framework of this social initiation, Leila undergoes a second (and in a way, more fundamental) initiation. This is her transition from childish innocence to adult awareness of the inevitable passing of time – an awareness so painful that it makes her want to opt out of this sophisticated world which is propelling her towards adulthood. Her longing for the safety of her rural home (**79** 7–10) shows how paralysing such knowledge can be: suddenly, she doesn't want to grow up. But though we can be sure that this knowledge will from now on always be part of her consciousness, it cannot be allowed to dominate. The end of the story sees Leila once again caught up in the excitement of the ball. Life goes on, and the old man's prophecy can take its course.

Characteristically of Mansfield's scrupulous art, we are not merely told about Leila's feelings but allowed to experience them from the inside. This restricted point of view is maintained so consistently that even descriptions of 'objective' facts and inanimate objects are filtered through Leila's consciousness and become themselves a measure of her emotional state. Katherine Mansfield's impressionistic sketch of Leila's "first ball" reflects an artistic perfection which is still unchallenged today.

Unit I
The Atmosphere and How it is Conveyed

Preparation: The students should have read the first two pages of the story.

1. Narrative style

*Comment on the amount of information in the first paragraph (**74** 1–6).*

[In all likelihood, some students will express their disappointment at the lack of concrete information about Leila and the situation she is in. They may think the narrator is indiscriminately confronting the reader with a random selection of things, while other perhaps more important details are missing.] Neither the cab nor its passengers nor the route are described in sufficient detail to satisfy one's curiosity. In addition, the paragraph contains a seemingly careless mixture of very specific ("the Sheridan girls and their brother", **74** 3) and extremely vague ("the ball", **74** 1) information. The main fact which emerges from all of this is that a young girl called Leila is sharing a cab with some others on the way to a ball.

2. Point of view and language

*From whose perspective do you think these lines were (**74** 1–6) written?*

[This question will probably make the students reconsider their first impressions and possibly modify any negative evaluation of the way the story is told.] It is obviously Leila's perspective. The first sentence refers to her thoughts, or more specifically, her confusion. The rest are mainly the impressions and feelings she had while sitting in the cab.

The narrator's choice of one central point of view only allows a limited amount of information which tends to be subjective in quality since reality is filtered, as it were, through Leila's consciousness.

Viewed in this light, both the selection of objects and the degree of concretization seem to exactly reflect the girl's mental processes, and especially her impatient anticipation of her dancing partners.

*How does the sentence "and away they bowled, past waltzing lamp-posts ..." (**74** 5–6) fit in with this observation? Consider also line 11.*

Since lamp-posts do not normally dance, this is obviously less a description of objective reality than of Leila's feelings: she is so carried away by her excitement that it seems to her the whole world is dancing with her. On the face of it, the rest of the sentence seems to contain a simple description of the cab's fast movement through the outskirts of a town. On closer scrutiny, however, it will be found that even this information is closely connected with Leila's present feelings. The emphatic word-order and the connotations of the verb ("away they bowled") also allude to Leila's excitement. This becomes even more palpable in the rhythm of the end of the sentence, where the words themselves are written in three-four waltz time:

∪	– ( ) ∪	– ∪ ∪	– ∪ ∪	– ∪ ∪	–
"past	waltzing	lamp-posts and	houses and	fences and	trees"

Line 11 is an exemple of 'interior monologue', i.e. a direct representation of Leila's actual thoughts, similar to reported speech but without any introductory 'she thought'. [Further examples: **74** 20; **74** 8–9; **77** 29–30; **78** 31–33, 34–35; **79** 1]

3. Atmosphere and point of view

How does Leila's present mood determine her vision of reality?

The girl's elation translates itself into a special vision of reality which, in turn, grants the reader a deeper insight into Leila's present mental state. In Leila's vivid imagination some objects around her begin to take on human features, becoming — like the waltzing lamp-posts already mentioned — themselves visitors to the ball, so to speak: cf. the "dancing" jet of gas that "could not wait", the "burst of tuning" that "leaped almost to the ceiling" (**75** 7–9), or the "talking" and "quivering" coloured flags (**75** 30–31). Characteristically, at this point everything seems to be in motion in sympathy with her. [Here the teacher should encourage the students to list the corresponding verbs and discuss their effects on the reader.]

The drill-hall and its interior are dipped into a gleaming light which, as if by a fairy-like magic, gilds the lanterns at the entrance, the polished floor, and even a dancer's head (**74** 33, **75** 37, **76** 35, **77** 22).

Everything is seen as being glamourous or cute: note the 'childish' over-use of the adjective "little", which makes it seem she is reducing everything to doll's house dimensions. Leila finds herself sitting "in her own little corner" of the cab (**74** 3), is aware of "Laura's little dark head" (**74** 13–14), notices "little satin shoes" (**74** 28) outside the hall, feels pushed into a "little room marked 'Ladies'" (**75** 1), sees people "trying to get at the little dressing-table and mirror" (**75** 5), watches "darling little pink-and-silver programmes" (**75** 20–21) tossed about, and, once in the ballroom, imagines the "little flags" to be talking (**75** 30). Not surprisingly then, Leila can be found naively marvelling at some things as being "so new" (**74** 12), "so great" (**75** 1, 28), or "so sweet" (**75** 36). She is so overwhelmed that she fails to register anything negative. Even the indifference of her companions (**74** 11) is seen as something admirable, and the "deafening" noise just adds to the excitement.

4. Effect of point of view on reader

How does it affect you when reading the story to see everything through Leila's eyes?

The advantages of this psychological approach are obvious. As well as experiencing the atmosphere of the ball as if we were there ourselves, we have, from the start, an intimate knowledge of Leila's situation. Since we are not diverted or prejudiced by any opposing point of view, we are strongly encouraged to sympathize with Leila.

Unit II
Social Conventions

1. Social conventions at the ball

What are the rules that seem to govern people's behaviour at the ball?

Leila enters a world whose most conspicuous characteristic is a net of rigid

conventions, to wit, people's unquestioned respect of certain rules of behaviour. The conventions of this ballroom world belong to the following categories:
Clothing, personal appearance: Both sexes are supposed to wear formal dress; for the young men, a dress-suit and gloves (**74** 5, 16–17); for the girls, elaborate dresses and hair-dos, lots of ribbons, flowers, frills and jewellary, velvet or fur cloaks, satin shoes, gloves, fans (**74** 13–14, 23–24, 28, 32; **75** 10–18, 37), Girls obviously feel they have to pay a lot of attention to their appearance, even to the extent of trying to conform to an 'ideal' female figure (**75** 10–11). The older women — the "chaperones" — are apparently all expected to wear "dark dresses" (**76** 1).
Ritualized behaviour: The dancing is not spontaneous, but planned at the start by entering names of partners into one's individual "programme" (**74** 19, **75** 19–24). The men and women stand in separate parts of the hall at the beginning. It is only the men who can choose their partners, and are accordingly expected to make the first move (**75** 19, **77** 8–20). The chaperones sit on the stage and do not take part in the dancing.
Conversation: It seems to be regarded as desirable to give the impression of being "indifferent" (**74** 11, cf. also **77** 11–12); though some moderately excited comments about their clothes and appearance are common among the girls (**75** 14–18). Conversation with one's dancing partner consists as a rule of stereotyped references to the quality of the floor, etc. (**76** 40, **77** 11, 29–30). This was probably conceived as a means with which to overcome one's awkwardness or embarrassment at the start of a new dance with a new partner.

2. Leila's attitude to the conventions of the ball
What does Leila think of these conventions?
From the outset, Leila has a strong desire to conform (**74** 11–12). She may be puzzled occasionally (**75** 22–23; **76** 6–9; **77** 31–32), but never doubts that it is eminently desirable to belong to this sophisticated society, and mastery of the rules of behaviour is a kind of passport. She seems to regard her "first ball" as a sort of sacred rite, an initiation into a new and better life (**77** 32–36).
How successful is Leila in her efforts to be accepted?
Being a novice to this adult world Leila is not always successful in her striving for conformity. For instance, her reference to the "slippery" quality of the floor (**77** 1) betrays unfamiliarity with the usual qualities of a dance-floor, and the terms normally used to describe it. In addition, both her confession that this is really her "first dance" (**77** 13, 30–31) and her

unchecked urge to talk about her social background, her country home (**77** 16–17), appear to be out of place on this occasion.
Consequently, her first partner finds her social inexperience puzzling (**77** 2–3) and finally reveals his consternation by growing taciturnity and little gestures of embarrassment (**77** 24–26). Similarly, her second partner is not interested in Leila's private 'story' either. Abruptly, and not very elegantly either, he suggests having an ice-cream (**77** 37) — another conventional ploy to cover one's embarrassment.

3. Free discussion
Do you think learning the rules of social behaviour is a necessary part of growing up?
Leila's occasional violations of conventional rules and the ensuing 'sanctions' may be seen as demonstrating the advantage of being at home with certain social conventions. Most likely, however, most students will denounce the conventionality depicted in the story as being destructive of any kind of spontaneity or sincerity, and thus ruling out real communication between people.
In order to prevent an unnecessary polarization the students could be asked to consider the 'conventions' that govern people's behaviour
— in the classroom
— at a football match
— in an 'alternative' pub or café
— at a political meeting
— in a disco
or any other situation familiar to them. The 'disco' situation offers the most promising parallels to the "ball" in the story (as described in Point 1). For all the apparent spontaneity, it is obvious that there are numerous conventions governing style of clothing, hairstyle, language (slang) and behaviour which are likely to make anyone unfamiliar with them feel awkward or out of place. Anyone who wants to 'belong' must first be 'initiated' into the rules of social behaviour — just like Leila at the ball.

4. The role of conventions in other stories [Optional]
In "Her First Ball", the idea of social conventions, and their observation or violation, is a major element. In other stories, e.g. "The Test" and "The Leapfrog Contest", this aspect of life is also relevant, though to a lesser extent. Say what the conventions are in each case, and what their role is in the story.
Homework: Re-read (or read to the end of) the story, and consider what Leila has learned by the end of her first ball.

Unit III
Leila's Initiation

1. The old man

In what ways does the old man differ from the other guests at the ball?

It seems to be unusual, but not quite against the rules of the game, for an elderly bachelor like this man to take part. In his appearance he compares unfavourably with the other men: "fat, with a big bald patch on his head" (**76** 17), his clothes "shabby", "creased" and "dusty" (**78** 4–5), and possibly in bad health (**78** 11). Leila is mildly shocked by the contrast: physically, her third dancing partner is exactly the opposite of the beauty and youth she has up to this moment identified with this ballroom world. He also differs in his behaviour; but this difference is more in his favour. In contrast with the banality of the girls' chatter (e.g. **74** 7–8), the young men's vanity (**76** 8–10) and their stereotyped comments to their dancing partners (**76** 40–**77** 14; **77** 29–32) he seems refreshingly human. His age not only makes him more observant (**78** 10–11) but also gives him the freedom to step outside the conventions of the ball and say what he really thinks (**78** 10–30).

2. Leila's reaction

How do his remarks affect Leila?

At first she is pleased that somebody is taking her seriously, instead of just exchanging platitudes (**78** 8–10). But what he says is that she herself will inevitably grow old — that her first ball is, by implication, just one more step on the road to the grave. It becomes clear that the old man's directness has deeply upset Leila. Probably without wanting to, he has destroyed her innocent and uncritical view of this ballroom world with a few pointed remarks.

For the first time we see Leila giving more than just a passing thought to the significance of her "first ball" within the context of her future life. Here, recognition and pain go hand in hand. She is ready to accept the truth of the old man's remark (**78** 31–33), but is almost overwhelmed by the sadness of it all (**78** 33–35). Then, however, sadness gives way to protest, as if she is rejecting the inevitability of the man's prophecy. In breaking off the dance, she is in effect saying, 'If this is what my first ball means, I don't want it'.

For a moment, she is like a child whose toy has been broken (**78** 40 – **79** 1). When she begins to long for the safety of her rural home (**79** 7–10), we see that she is now afraid of growing up.

3. The ending and its significance

In what mood does Leila continue the ball?

Leila's rejection of the ball is of short duration. A bit later she is once again enjoying her next dance, enthralled by the seductive music, the swift movement and the splendour of the ballroom (**79** 11–16), all of which help her to forget the old man's jarring words. Significantly, she does not even recognize the old man when she encounters him a third time (**79** 16–18).

How does the ending relate to the old man's prophecy? It suggests that he is very probably right. For his prophecy to come true, Leila *must* be caught up again in the excitement of this and many other balls, fall in love, get married, have children of her own, etc.

4. Summing up: Leila's double initiation

Do you think she really has forgotten the old man's words?

Most likely she has for the moment merely suppressed her awareness of the unpleasant truth. Once 'initiated' into an awareness of the inevitable passage of time, she is not likely to forget it completely: in quieter moments of her life it will probably come back to her. But for the moment it would interfere with the business of living. [One could raise the question here what the effect would be on our lives if we were to be constantly thinking of death.]

So at the end of the story, Leila's 'social initiation' (cf. Unit II) takes precedence again. For all its artificiality, the world of the ball is helping her on her way to adulthood.

5. Comparison with "His First Flight" [Optional]

In what way is Leila's initiation similar to the young seagull's in "His First Flight"? What are the differences?

British and Non-British Pronunciation

In the annotations, the standard British pronunciation (R.P.) is given. Since so many of the stories are, however, spoken on the accompanying cassette by non-British speakers, an indication is given in the table opposite of the main differences in each case. Blanks imply no significant deviation from R.P. The equally important differences in intonation cannot, of course, be indicated here.

British (R.P.) "The Speech"		American "Charles" "The Princess and the Tin Box"		Irish "The Captive Princess" "His First Flight"		Australian "The Pepper-Tree"	
[ɒ]	not, what	[ɑ]	stop, box				
[æ]	man, cab	[æ]	hat laugh, class	[æ] - [a]	man, sad castle	[æ] - [a]	man branch
[ɑ:]	glass, laugh father yard, party	[ɑ:]	father	[ɑ:]	father	[ɑ:]	father, ask backyard
		[ɑr]	far, heart	[ɑr]	hard		
[ə]	member	[ər]	daughter	[ər]	sister		
[ɪə]	hear	[ir]	here	[ir]	year, clear		
[ʊə] - [ɔ:]	sure	[ʊr]	poor	[ʊr]	your		
[ɔ:] - [ɔə]	more	[or]	door	[or]	door, before		
	(similar difference between other vowels ending in 'r')						
[əʊ]	those, no	[oʊ]	spoke	[oʊ] - [o:]	no, close	[aʊ] - [ʌʊ]	soul, spoke
[aɪ]	crime					[aɪ] - [ɔɪ]	aside
[eɪ]	say			[eɪ] - [e:]	haste, delay	[ʌɪ] - [aɪ]	wait
[i:]	speech					[ʌi:]	leaves
[u:]	do					[ʌʊ]	too
[ju:]	duty	[u:] - [ju:]	Tuesday				
[w]	what	[hw]	what	[hw]	whine, whirlpool		
[t]	Peter, might	[*voiceless* 'd'] *(between vowels)*	Saturday	[*fricative* 't'] *(between vowels, end position)*	water, coat	[*voiceless* 'd'] *(between vowels)*	city
[θ]	threat, thick			[θ] - [t]	thick, northwards		
[ð]	father			[ð] - [d]	feather, smooth		

Index to Themes Dealt with in the Teaching Units

The stories are here referred to by the numbers used in the table on page 11. Numbers in bold print indicate an extended treatment of the aspect in question.

Bibliography

Abrams, M.H., *A Glossary of Literary Terms,* Third edition, New York 1971

Barmeyer, Eike (ed.), *Science Fiction: Theorie und Geschichte,* UTB 132, Munich 1972

Berkman, Sylvia, *Katherine Mansfield: A Critical Study,* Yale University Press, New Haven, Conn. 1959

Brooks, Cleanth/Warren, Robert Penn, *Understanding Fiction,* Second edition, Englewood Cliffs, N.J. 1971

Daly, Saralyn, *Katherine Mansfield,* Twayne's English Autors Series, New York 1965

Elliot, Brian, "Stivens, Dal(las George)" in: James Vinson, *Contemporary Novelists,* Second edition, London 1976, pp. 1303–1305

Floan, Howard R., *William Saroyan,* Twayne's U.S. Authors Series, New York 1966

Freese, Peter, "Die Short Story im Englischunterricht der Sekundarstufe II: Entwurf eines Interpretationsverfahrens" in: *Der Fremdsprachliche Unterricht* No. 1/1976 (Heft 37), pp. 2–15

Freese, Peter/Groene, Horst/Hermes, Liesel (eds.), *Die Short Story im Englischunterricht der Sekundarstufe II: Theorie und Praxis,* Informationen zur Sprach- und Literaturdidaktik Bd. 23, Schöningh, Paderborn 1979

Friedman, Lenemaja, *Shirley Jackson,* Twayne's U.S. Authors Series, New York 1975

Goetsch, Paul, *Studien und Materialien zur Short Story,* Schule und Forschung Bd. 15, Diesterweg, Frankfurt am Main 1971

Holmes, Charles S. (ed.), *Thurber: A Collection of Critical Essays* (Twentieth-century Views), Prentice Hall, Englewood Cliffs, N.J.

Kelly, Angeline A., *Liam O'Flaherty the Storyteller,* Macmillan, London 1976

O'Brien, James H., *Liam O'Flaherty* (Irish Writers Series), Bucknell University Press, Lewisburg, Pa. 1973

Rabkin, Eric S. (ed.), *Fantastic Worlds: Myths, Tales, and Stories,* OUP, Oxford and New York 1979

Saul, George Brandon, "Strange Gods and Far Places: The Short Stories of Lord Dunsany" in: *American Quarterly* XIX (1963), pp. 197–210

Scott, Virgil/Madden, David, *Studies in the Short Story,* Fifth edition by David Madden, New York, Chicago and San Francisco 1980

Stockebrand, Matthias/Nadorf, Bernhard, "Unterrichtsschritte auf dem Weg zur selbständig angefertigten Interpretation von erzählenden Texten" in: *Der Fremdsprachliche Unterricht* No. 3/1982 (Heft 64), pp. 295–305

Tobias, Richard C., *The Art of James Thurber,* Ohio University Press, Athens, Ohio 1969

Walter, Heribert, "Das Strukturdiagramm als Interpretationshilfe im Englischunterricht", in: *Der Fremdsprachliche Unterricht* No. 4/1982 (Heft 64), pp. 258–269

Weiand, Hermann, I. (ed.), *Insight V: Analyses of Twentieth-Century British and American Fiction,* Hirschgraben, Frankfurt am Main 1981